THE SCIENCE OF COLLECTIONS

DRIVING FINANCIAL SUCCESS IN BANKING AND NBFCS

Transforming the Collections Paradigm - Integrating Strategy, Technology, and Collaborating to Elevate Portfolio Quality in Banking and Financial Services

VIJAY VASUDEVAN

ISBN
Hardcase 979-8-89724-906-0
Paperback 979-8-89699-914-0

Contents

❖   Contents   ❖

In the timeless verses of the **Kamba Ramayana**, there is a profound sloka that resonates deeply with the complexities of debt and its impact on human emotions:

"Kadan pattar nenjam pol kalangidum, Udan pirandhar vanjanai thaan undhanukku."

This translates to, *"The heart of one in debt is always unsettled, like the deceit of a close relative weighs on you."* These words from the ancient epic beautifully capture the burden and inner turmoil experienced by those who are indebted. Debt, as depicted here, is not merely a financial obligation but a weight that unsettles the mind and challenges one's emotional and moral balance.

In the modern context of banking and financial services, this wisdom offers a crucial insight: managing debt is not just about numbers or recovery targets; it is about understanding the human side of financial obligations. By acknowledging the emotional strain debt causes and adopting customer-centric approaches to lending and collections, financial institutions can drive both financial success and societal well-being.

This book, *The Science of Collections: Driving Financial Success in Banking and NBFCs*, is inspired by such timeless wisdom, marrying it with contemporary strategies and technologies. It underscores the importance of ethical, empathetic, and data-driven practices in ensuring that collections are not just effective but also humane. After all, the heart of every financial transaction is the customer, and their well-being is the foundation of sustainable growth.

Foreword

It is with great honour and pleasure that I write the foreword for The Science of Collections, a remarkable work by Vijay Vasudevan, a professional I have had the privilege of mentoring and collaborating with for over eight years at Tata Motors Finance. During this period, Vijay played a pivotal role in transforming the collections landscape of the organization, leading the Centre of Excellence, and achieving remarkable milestones through his relentless pursuit of innovation, strategy, and execution.

Under my guidance, Vijay spearheaded the design and development of an end-to-end collections and legal solution called Lakshmi, a groundbreaking system that earned intellectual property rights for Tata Motors Finance. Vijay's vision and expertise ensured that Lakshmi became a cornerstone of the organization's collections strategy, blending advanced technology, analytics, and operational excellence. This achievement is a testament to his deep understanding of collections processes, his ability to think strategically, and his commitment to delivering results. His coding and programming skills further helped in developing Lakshmi.

Drawing on his 25+ years of extensive experience—from managing field collections to heading the Centre of Excellence,

Vijay brings unparalleled insights into the science and art of collections. His journey has been one of continuous learning, innovation, and impact, and this book is a culmination of that journey. It encapsulates his practical expertise, strategic mindset, and a deep understanding of the evolving financial landscape.

The Book's Value and Features

The Science of Collections is much more than a guide—it is a blueprint for excellence in collections keeping in mind the current regulatory landscape for NBFCs and banks. It meticulously addresses every aspect of collections, providing actionable insights and strategic frameworks for professionals in the banking and financial services sector. Vijay delves into the nuances of collections with topics like:

- Building Robust Collections Strategies: A structured approach to defining and executing collections processes within the current regulatory and legal ambit.

- Effective Models and Execution: Harnessing the power of data to drive efficiencies and optimize performance.

- Advanced Analytics and Technology: Leveraging AI, predictive analytics, and automation to enhance collections outcomes.

- Cross-Functional Collaboration: Emphasizing the role of teamwork across collections, customer service, legal, and strategy functions.

- Leadership and Preparing for the Future: Insights into leading high-performance teams and adapting to the changing collections landscape.

- Customer First – He covers customer behaviour and how to manage the same. Follow up strategies are defined with emphasis on empathetic behaviour to ensure customer trust at all times.

Vijay's comprehensive coverage of key topics, from pre-delinquency management to advanced metrics and compliance, makes this book a valuable resource for professionals across collections, operations, customer service, business intelligence, and strategy teams. The inclusion of case studies, FAQs, and a glossary ensures that readers not only learn but also find practical solutions to common challenges in the collections domain.

A Must-Read for the Industry

In today's complex financial environment with a tight regulatory framework, collections is no longer just an operational necessity—it is a strategic imperative. Vijay's book redefines collections as a sophisticated, data-driven discipline, capable of driving both financial stability and customer trust. The Science of Collections is a must-read for anyone involved in the collections ecosystem, from field agents and operations managers to strategists and senior executives.

As someone who has witnessed Vijay's dedication, leadership, and ingenuity firsthand, I am confident that this book will serve as a guiding light for professionals and organizations aiming to elevate their collections processes.

I wholeheartedly recommend The Science of Collections to anyone seeking to master the art and science of collections. Vijay's expertise, combined with his passion for innovation, makes this book a valuable contribution to the financial services industry.

— Alok Chadha
Former Executive Director and Chief Operating Officer,
Tata Motors Finance Limited

Preface

In the dynamic and ever-evolving world of banking and financial services, the collections process has often been perceived as a straightforward operational activity recovering overdue payments through field agents and external agencies. However, over two decades of immersive, hands-on experience in the field, I have come to see collections as much more than that.

My journey in collections has taken me through diverse roles, from the ground-level responsibilities of managing field operations to heading Collections Strategy and the Centre of Excellence (CoE) for leading banks and non-banking financial companies (NBFCs). These years have offered me a unique perspective and a deep understanding of the intricacies of collections, spanning strategy, execution, and technology adoption.

One of the pivotal milestones in my career has been the design and development of a comprehensive, end-to-end collections strategy system; a framework so robust and effective that it is now intellectual property. This system was built to address the critical gaps I observed in the traditional collections approach. It integrates data-driven decision-making, advanced technology, and seamless collaboration between stakeholders to create a powerful tool that optimizes recovery rates and portfolio performance.

This book reflects my belief that collections should no longer be seen as an isolated or reactive function. Instead, it should be approached as a sophisticated, proactive, and collaborative process that plays a vital role in maintaining portfolio quality and ensuring financial stability. Through these pages, I share insights and methodologies that challenge the traditional, siloed view of collections and provide a roadmap to transform it into a streamlined and effective discipline.

Drawing from my extensive experience, this book advocates for a holistic collections strategy that aligns the efforts of Collections, Customer Service, Residual Management, Legal, and Insurance teams. With technology as the backbone, the approach emphasizes predictive analytics, integrated workflows, and an enhanced focus on customer engagement. The actionable strategies and frameworks presented here are designed to guide financial institutions toward building collections processes that are scalable, customer-centric, and future-ready.

I have also woven real-world experiences and case studies throughout the book to highlight how theory translates into practice. These examples reflect the challenges I have faced and the solutions I have implemented, often breaking new ground in the collections domain.

Whether you are a collection professional, a strategist, or a decision-maker in banking or NBFCs, this book will equip you with the knowledge and tools to elevate your collections efforts. My hope is that it serves as a resource to help you unlock the true potential of collections—not just as a recovery mechanism but as a driver of financial resilience and customer trust.

As we advance into a future defined by innovation and heightened customer expectations, rethinking collections is not just an opportunity—it is an imperative. Together, we can redefine the art and science of collections into a discipline that ensures financial stability, strengthens customer relationships, and fosters long-term success for organizations.

— Vijay Vasudevan

01

Understanding the Collections Landscape

Collections is a cornerstone of financial institutions, balancing the recovery of overdue payments with preserving customer relationships and ensuring long-term financial health. As an author with extensive experience in collections strategy, I aim to unravel the complexities of this vital function. This chapter delves into its evolution, significance, and the ecosystem of stakeholders involved, offering readers a comprehensive understanding of the collections landscape.

1.1 The Evolution of Collections in Banking and NBFCs

The collections process has undergone a remarkable transformation over the years, driven by advancements in technology, regulatory changes, and shifting customer expectations.

- **Traditional Collections:** In the early days, collections were rudimentary and manual. Financial institutions primarily relied on personal visits and physical notices to recover overdue amounts. This process was labour-intensive, costly, and often inefficient, with little room for segmentation or strategy.

- **Technological Advancements:** The introduction of banking software in the 1980s and 1990s revolutionized collections by enabling basic portfolio tracking and automation. The emergence of credit bureaus further empowered banks and NBFCs to assess customer creditworthiness and predict delinquency patterns.

- **The Digital Era:** The rise of digital channels and data analytics has redefined collections as a science. Institutions now leverage advanced algorithms to segment customers based on behaviour and risk profiles. Automation, voice bots, and omnichannel communication have streamlined interactions, making collections less intrusive and more efficient.

The Future of Collections

Today, collections are evolving into a customer-centric function. Predictive analytics, artificial intelligence (AI), and machine learning (ML) are enabling institutions to anticipate payment difficulties and intervene proactively. This evolution underscores a shift from a reactive to a proactive and empathetic approach.

1.2   The Role of Collections in Bank's Success

Collections is not just about recovering money; it is a pivotal function that ensures the financial stability and profitability of banks and NBFCs.

- **Preserving Asset Quality:** Collections play a critical role in maintaining asset quality by minimizing delinquencies and non-performing assets (NPAs).

An effective collections strategy ensures timely interventions, preventing accounts from slipping into higher delinquency buckets.

- **Enhancing Cash Flow:** Steady and consistent collections are essential for maintaining liquidity. A robust collections process ensures that funds are reinvested, supporting lending activities and growth.

- **Building Customer Relationships:** Modern collections emphasize customer engagement. By offering support and flexible repayment options, institutions can foster trust and loyalty, transforming collections into an opportunity to strengthen customer relationships.

- **Mitigating Risks:** An efficient collections process reduces credit risks by identifying and addressing potential defaults early. It also ensures compliance with regulatory requirements, protecting institutions from penalties and reputational damage.

1.3 Key Stakeholders in the Collections Process

The success of a collections strategy hinges on the collaboration of various stakeholders, each playing a distinct yet interconnected role.

- **Customers:** Customers are at the center of the collections process. Understanding their financial behaviour, challenges, and preferences is critical for designing effective strategies. A customer-centric approach ensures that interventions are empathetic and solution-oriented.

- **Collections Teams:** These include in-house collections executives, field agents, and outsourced agencies. Their role is to execute the collections strategy, whether through phone calls, digital nudges, or in-person visits. Performance metrics like resolution rates and rollbacks are key to evaluating their effectiveness.

- **Customer Service Teams:** Customer service complements collections by addressing queries and resolving disputes. Seamless coordination between these teams ensures a smoother collections process and enhances customer satisfaction.

- **Credit and Risk Teams:** Credit and risk teams provide the analytical backbone for collections. They develop customer risk scores and segment portfolios, enabling tailored interventions. Their insights guide the allocation of resources and the prioritization of accounts.

- **Legal and Compliance Teams:** Legal teams handle escalated cases requiring litigation or arbitration, while compliance teams ensure that the collections process adheres to regulatory standards. Their involvement safeguards the institution's reputation and minimizes legal risks.

- **Technology Teams:** Technology teams develop and manage the tools and platforms that drive collections, from customer relationship management (CRM) systems to voice bots and analytics dashboards. Their role is crucial in automating processes and ensuring scalability.

- **Leadership and Strategy Teams:** The leadership team sets the vision for collections, balancing financial goals with customer-centric values. Strategy teams translate this vision into actionable plans, integrating technological solutions and performance metrics to optimize outcomes.

Understanding the collections landscape is essential for appreciating its role in the success of financial institutions. The evolution of collections reflects broader changes in the banking and NBFC sectors, highlighting the increasing importance of technology, data-driven decision-making, and customer-centricity. By involving a diverse group of stakeholders, institutions can create a robust collections framework that not only ensures financial stability but also builds long-term customer trust. This chapter sets the stage for exploring advanced strategies and tools that can transform collections from a reactive process into a proactive, relationship-building function.

The Science Behind Collections

Collections is no longer a process driven by intuition or mere operational routines—it has evolved into a sophisticated discipline rooted in science. Understanding the factors that influence customer behaviour, leveraging data for precision, and tailoring strategies to individual borrower profiles are the pillars of modern collections. This chapter explores how behavioural economics helps decode borrower psychology, how analytics empowers institutions with actionable insights, and how segmentation transforms collections from generic approaches to personalized engagements. By applying these scientific principles, financial institutions can not only enhance recovery rates but also build stronger relationships with their customers, making collections a cornerstone of sustainable financial success.

2.1 Understanding Borrower Psychology

The foundation of effective collections lies in understanding why borrowers act the way they do. Behavioural economics sheds light on the psychology behind financial decision-making, offering valuable insights into repayment behaviour. Borrowers are not a monolithic group; their actions are influenced by a variety of factors—emotional, social, and economic. Some miss payments due to temporary setbacks, others prioritize different obligations, and a few may even resist repayment intentionally.

To address this diversity, portfolio bifurcation becomes essential. By categorizing borrowers based on risk and behavioural scores, financial institutions can implement targeted strategies that align with the underlying psychology of each segment. Portfolio bifurcation is not just about organizing accounts; it's a behavioural science-driven tool to maximize efficiency, engagement, and recovery outcomes.

2.2   Data-Driven Collections: The Power of Analytics

Collections in modern financial institutions is no longer just a numbers game—it's a data game. Data analytics transforms collections from reactive to proactive. By analysing repayment trends, customer interactions, and external credit bureau data, institutions can anticipate delinquencies before they occur.

Advanced analytics enable financial institutions to:

- **Predict Risk**: Understand the likelihood of delinquency through predictive modelling.

- **Optimize Engagement**: Identify the best communication channels and timing for different borrower profiles.

- **Allocate Resources**: Prioritize high-risk accounts while automating reminders for low-risk ones.

Data-driven collections go together with behavioural economics by using evidence-based insights to tailor interactions, ensuring that recovery strategies are both effective and empathetic.

2.3   Segmentation Strategies

Gone are the days of one-size-fits-all collections strategies. Modern borrowers demand personalization, and segmentation is the key to achieving it. By dividing the portfolio into distinct categories based on risk, behaviour, and demographic data, institutions can engage borrowers in a way that resonates with their unique circumstances.

Evolving from Generic to Personalized Segmentation

- **Generic Approaches**: Treat all delinquent borrowers the same, relying on mass communication and standardized recovery strategies.

- **Personalized Approaches**: Use multidimensional scoring to segment borrowers, tailoring communication and intervention methods for each group.

Benefits of Personalized Segmentation

- **Higher Recovery Rates**: Engaging borrowers with strategies that address their specific challenges increases the likelihood of repayment.

- **Improved Customer Experience**: Personalized approaches demonstrate empathy, enhancing trust and long-term loyalty.

- **Operational Efficiency**: Focused efforts reduce wasted resources on low-risk accounts and streamline attention to high-risk segments.

By combining behavioural economics, data analytics, and robust segmentation strategies, financial institutions can transform collections from a reactive recovery process to a proactive and strategic initiative. These approaches don't just drive financial success—they strengthen relationships with borrowers, ensuring mutual growth and resilience.

03

Building Robust Collections Strategy

In the banking and financial services sector, the collections strategy is one of the most critical components of portfolio management. It is not merely a reactive function to recover overdue payments but a proactive approach to safeguarding the portfolio's quality, minimizing credit losses, and maintaining customer trust. A well-structured collections strategy integrates customer understanding, advanced technologies, and operational excellence to ensure maximum efficiency and effectiveness.

A. Aligning Collections with Business Goals

The collections strategy must align seamlessly with the organization's broader business objectives.

- **Portfolio Quality Management**: The primary aim is to maintain a healthy portfolio by reducing delinquency rates and ensuring timely recoveries.

- **Profitability and Cost Optimization**: The strategy should focus on recovering overdue amounts while minimizing operational costs, such as field visits and legal actions.

- **Customer Retention and Relationship Management**: Collections should balance empathy and efficiency to ensure that customers feel supported rather than alienated. This is especially critical in competitive markets where customer satisfaction is paramount.

- **Regulatory Compliance**: Adherence to fair lending practices, data protection regulations, and other compliance norms must be embedded in the strategy.

B. Customer-Centric Collections: Balancing Empathy with Efficiency

An effective collections strategy recognizes that each customer is unique. By adopting a customer-centric approach, financial institutions can better manage collections while preserving relationships.

Key Elements of Customer-Centric Collections

- **Segmentation and Profiling**:
  - Use data to segment customers based on risk levels, repayment history, and financial behaviour.
  - Create customer personas to predict their likely responses to different collection approaches.

- **Personalized Engagement**:
  - Tailor communication channels and messages to individual customer preferences (e.g., SMS, email, calls).
  - Provide flexible repayment options for customers facing genuine financial hardships.

- **Empathetic Communication**:

  - Train collection agents to listen to customer concerns and offer solutions rather than pressuring them for payments.

  - Use scripts and role-playing exercises to build rapport and trust.

C. Developing a Holistic Collections Framework

A robust collections strategy is built on a comprehensive framework that integrates key operational, technological, and analytical components.

3.1 Risk Segmentation

Segmenting the portfolio into distinct categories based on risk levels, delinquency stages, and customer profiles allows for a more targeted approach.

- **Risk-Based Segmentation**: Divide customers into buckets (e.g., low, medium, and high risk) using credit scoring and repayment behaviour.

- **Bucket Classification**: Classify accounts based on the number of days past due (DPD) for prioritized interventions (e.g., 1-30 DPD, 31-60 DPD, 60+ DPD).

3.2 Right Allocation Logic Execution

Effective allocation of accounts to collectors is a cornerstone of a successful collections strategy.

- **Customer-Level Allocation**: Ensure that all accounts related to the same customer are handled by one collector to avoid duplicate efforts.

- **Collector Performance Metrics**: Assign cases based on collector expertise, historical performance, and geographical knowledge.

- **Dynamic Allocation**: Use AI and rule engines to reassign cases dynamically based on changing customer circumstances or collector performance.

3.3 Measuring the Right Performance

Key performance indicators (KPIs) must be tracked to assess the success of the collections strategy.

- **Roll Rate Reduction**: Measure the movement of accounts from one delinquency bucket to another.

- **Resolution Rate**: Track the percentage of overdue accounts resolved within specific timeframes.

- **Recovery Rate**: Assess the percentage of overdue amounts recovered relative to the total overdue.

- **Productivity Metrics**: Monitor collector efficiency using metrics such as calls made, visits completed, and payments collected.

3.4 Tracking Productivity

- **Field Dispositions**: Ensure that field agents provide detailed, standardized feedback after each interaction to improve strategy refinement.

- **Subjective Feedback Analysis**: Use text analytics and sentiment analysis to derive actionable insights from subjective field feedback.

3.4.1　Integrating Advanced Technologies

Technology is the backbone of a modern collections strategy.

- **Artificial Intelligence (AI)**: Predict delinquency risk using machine learning models, Automate reminders and payment follow-ups for low-risk customers.

- **Rule Engines**: Create dynamic workflows based on predefined rules to prioritize cases and allocate resources efficiently.

- **Location Intelligence**: Use geospatial analytics to optimize field visits, reduce travel time, and enhance collector productivity.

- **Data Science**: Analyse historical repayment patterns and external data (e.g., macroeconomic indicators) to refine strategies.

- **Omni-Channel Platforms**: Provide customers with seamless communication across multiple channels, enabling them to interact at their convenience.

- **Digital Payment Tools**: Offer customers easy-to-use digital payment options to settle their dues quickly and conveniently.

4.1 Strategies for Implementing Collections at Scale

- **Pilot Testing**: Start with small, controlled deployments to evaluate the effectiveness of new strategies.

- **Scalability Planning**: Build frameworks and technologies that can handle increased case volumes as the portfolio grows.

- **Feedback Loops**: Incorporate feedback from customers and collectors to continuously refine the strategy.

5.1 Continuous Monitoring and Optimization

- Conduct periodic audits to ensure adherence to the strategy.

- Use dashboards and real-time analytics to identify trends and adjust tactics.

- Regularly review and update risk models to keep pace with changing customer behaviours and market dynamics.

A robust collections strategy is not just about recovering overdue payments; it is about building a resilient, customer-centric, and technologically advanced framework that supports the organization's long-term goals. By aligning collections with business objectives, balancing empathy with efficiency, and leveraging cutting-edge technologies, financial institutions can protect their portfolios while fostering trust and loyalty among customers. This strategic approach positions collections not as a challenge but as an opportunity for growth, innovation, and sustainable success.

Laying the Foundation for Superior Collections

"A strong foundation in collections is built on clarity, strategy, and unwavering execution. It's not just about recovering dues but about building trust, relationships, and long-term financial health."

— Vijay Vasudevan

04

Effective Portfolio Bifurcation Using Power of Data

Portfolio bifurcation is the cornerstone of any successful collections strategy. It involves segmenting the portfolio into distinct categories based on customer risk and behaviour scores. This segmentation enables banks and financial institutions to allocate resources effectively, prioritize recovery efforts, and optimize the collections process.

Key Components of Portfolio Bifurcation

1. **Customer-Level Analysis**

   - **Repayment History:** Analysing the borrower's repayment trends, such as missed payments, delays, or consistent adherence to payment schedules.

   - **Market Behaviour:** Examining whether the borrower is repaying loans from other lenders while defaulting on the current institution's loans, using insights from credit bureau data.

   - **Behaviour Scoring:** Assigning a risk and behaviour score based on repayment history, external market data, and predictive analytics.

2. **Customer Segment Analysis**

   - Identifying how borrowers with similar profiles (e.g., occupation, income bracket, loan size) perform within the portfolio.

   - Highlighting patterns within specific customer groups to determine which segments are more prone to delinquency or timely repayment.

3. **Product-Level Analysis**

   - Assessing the performance of individual loan products in the portfolio.

   - Understanding which products are generating higher delinquency or NPA percentages and identifying their unique risk factors.

4. **Geographic Analysis**

   - Mapping delinquency ratios and NPA percentages across various locations.

   - Highlighting geographic areas with higher risk exposure, enabling targeted recovery efforts.

5. **Multidimensional Scoring**

   - Using a combination of the above parameters—customer behaviour, product performance, geographic insights, and credit bureau data—to calculate a final risk and behaviour score.

   - This score provides a probability assessment of a borrower going into delinquency or maintaining a good repayment record.

Steps in Portfolio Bifurcation

1. **Behaviour Scoring**

   - Assign a behaviour score to each customer by analysing repayment patterns, credit bureau insights, and customer-level factors.

   - The behaviour score helps categorize customers into risk brackets such as Low Risk, Moderate Risk, and High Risk.

2. **Delinquency Segmentation**

   - Segment accounts based on Days Past Due (DPD), such as:

     - **0–30 DPD:** Early-stage accounts, requiring soft reminders.

     - **31–90 DPD:** Mid-stage accounts, needing assertive follow-ups.

     - **91+ DPD:** Late-stage accounts, potentially requiring legal intervention.

3. **Portfolio Mapping**

   - Combine customer-level behaviour scores and DPD segmentation to create actionable categories. For instance:

     - High-Risk Customers in Early Delinquency

     - Low-Risk Customers in Late Delinquency

4. **Final Bifurcation and Allocation**

- Allocate accounts based on their segmented category to field agents, tele callers, or legal teams.

- Prioritize high-risk accounts for immediate action and low-risk accounts for monitoring and automated reminders.

Portfolio bifurcation is the first and most crucial step in the collections process. It lays the groundwork for effective allocation and recovery strategies by providing a detailed understanding of customer risk and behaviour. The next chapters will explore advanced topics such as behaviour scoring models and allocation strategies, building on the foundation of portfolio bifurcation.

05

Logical Allocation of Accounts

In collections, allocation is more than just distributing delinquent cases among field executives and agencies. It is a critical part of the collections strategy that directly impacts the efficiency and effectiveness of recovery efforts. As I often say, **"Effective and Right Allocation ensures 50% of Collections Performance."** This principle has been proven through my practical experience heading collections strategy.

Many organizations fail to harness the potential of effective allocation by focusing on delinquent accounts in isolation and neglecting the broader customer profile. This leads to inefficiencies, duplication of efforts, and suboptimal recovery outcomes. An effective allocation process should be designed to ensure that the right accounts are assigned to the right people, with a focus on both the customer and collector profiles.

5.1   Challenges in Traditional Allocation Methods

1. **Account-Level Allocation**

   - Accounts are allocated based on delinquency (DPD) levels rather than considering the customer's overall loan profile.

   - Customers with multiple loan products across different delinquency buckets are often assigned to multiple collection executives, leading to redundant efforts and field-level confusion.

2. **Area-Based Allocation**

   - Allocation is frequently done based on the geographical reach of field staff or agencies without factoring in customer risk or collector performance.

   - This approach disregards the expertise or track record of the assigned collectors.

3. **Lack of Integration in Customer View**

   o   Banks and NBFCs often fail to consider a customer's complete loan portfolio, including performing accounts, when allocating delinquent accounts.

   o   This siloed approach leads to missed opportunities for early resolution and better customer management.

5.2   Principles of Effective Allocation

1. **Allocate at the Customer Level**

   o   Treat the customer, not the account, as the primary unit of allocation.

   o   Consolidate all accounts (delinquent and performing) under a single customer profile and assign them to one collection executive.

2. **Behaviour-Driven Allocation**

   o   Use customer behaviour scores (based on repayment history, risk profile, and predictive analytics) to determine priority and assign cases accordingly.

   o   For instance:

      ▪   **Very High Risk (VH)** and **High Risk (H)** customers should be prioritized and handled by the best-performing executives.

      ▪   **Low Risk (L)** and **Very Low Risk (VL)** customers can be managed through automated reminders or less experienced staff.

3. **Collector Performance Metrics**

   o Evaluate collectors based on their productivity scores, calculated using the following parameters:

     ▪ Historical performance in resolving cases.

     ▪ Rollback and normalization rates (ability to reduce DPD levels).

     ▪ Average customer visits per day.

     ▪ Timeliness of resolution (avoiding end-of-month rush).

     ▪ Customer service orientation and compliance with protocols.

   o Classify collectors as:

     ▪ **E - Excellent**

     ▪ **S - Satisfactory**

     ▪ **A - Average Performer**

     ▪ **U - Under Performer**

4. **Matching Customer and Collector Profiles**

   o Align customer behaviour scores with collector performance ratings:

     ▪ **Very High Risk (VH)** and **High Risk (H)** customers → **Excellent (E)** collectors.

     ▪ **Medium Risk (M)** customers → **Satisfactory (S)** collectors.

- **Low Risk (L)** and **Very Low Risk (VL)** customers → **Average (A)** or **Under Performer (U)** collectors, depending on automation feasibility.

5. **Dynamic Allocation**

   - Continuously update allocation based on new data, such as payment updates, customer interactions, or changes in collector performance.

5.3 Proposed Allocation Framework

Customer Behaviour Score	Collector Rating	Allocation Priority	Objective
Very High Risk (VH)	Excellent (E)	Immediate and intensive follow-up	Maximize recovery, prevent further defaults
High Risk (H)	Excellent (E)	High priority	Address early signs of financial distress
Medium Risk (M)	Satisfactory (S)	Moderate priority	Ensure timely intervention
Low Risk (L)	Average (A)	Low priority	Maintain customer relationship
Very Low Risk (VL)	Under Performer (U) or automation	Automated reminders or minimal effort	Monitor and ensure compliance

5.4   Benefits of Strategic Allocation

1. **Improved Productivity**

   - Minimizes duplication of efforts by assigning all accounts of a single customer to one collector.

   - Optimizes the workload of field staff based on their expertise and past performance.

2. **Higher Recovery Rates**

   - Allocating high-risk accounts to experienced collectors ensures better resolution rates.

3. **Enhanced Customer Experience**

   - A unified approach reduces customer confusion and friction, improving their experience even during delinquency.

4. **Cost Efficiency**

   - Reduces redundant visits and resource wastage.

   - Enables better planning and allocation of resources.

5. **Data-Driven Decision Making**

   - Allows for continuous refinement of allocation strategies based on real-time performance data.

Effective allocation is not merely an operational task—it is a strategic initiative that drives collections performance. By focusing on customer-level allocation and aligning it with collector performance metrics, banks and NBFCs can achieve significant improvements in recovery rates, operational efficiency, and customer satisfaction. The next chapter will delve deeper into the behaviour scoring model and its role in shaping allocation strategies.

06

Maintaining Account Coverage Ratio (ACR) in Allocations

Account Coverage Ratio (ACR) is a crucial metric in the allocation process, representing the number of accounts assigned to each collection executive. Striking the right balance in ACR is essential for ensuring optimal performance and productivity.

6.1 Impact of ACR on Performance

1. **Overloaded ACR:**

   - Assigning too many accounts to a single executive dilutes their focus, leading to delayed follow-ups and suboptimal recovery rates.

   - Overburdening results in collector fatigue, reducing their effectiveness and motivation.

2. **Underutilized ACR:**

   - Assigning fewer accounts than an executive can handle leads to inefficiency and increased cost per recovery.

   - This creates idle time and reduces the overall productivity of the team.

Recommended ACR Levels

- **X Bucket (Early Delinquency):** 70-80 accounts per executive. 700 customer per call center caller

- **30+ DPD Cases (Mid/High Delinquency):** 50 accounts per executive, due to the higher complexity and intensive follow-ups required.

6.2   Challenges of Maintaining ACR

One of the biggest challenges in collections is the sudden flow of cases from lower buckets to higher buckets, which can disrupt the ACR balance. Such surges can occur due to:

- Seasonal variations in repayment behaviour.

- Economic factors affecting borrower cash flows.

- Inefficiencies in early delinquency collections, leading to rollovers into higher buckets.

6.3   Contingency Plans for Managing ACR

1. **Dynamic Workforce Scaling**

   o **Pool of On-Call Collectors:** Maintain a roster of part-time or on-call collection executives who can step in during high-volume periods.

   o **Flexible Agency Contracts:** Partner with agencies that can provide additional resources during spikes in case flows.

2. **Technology-Driven Support**

   o **Automated Communications:** Use digital tools to handle early-stage delinquencies (e.g., SMS, IVR, or app notifications) to reduce manual intervention.

   o **AI-Powered Prioritization:** Leverage predictive analytics to prioritize high-risk cases for immediate allocation, while low-risk cases can be scheduled for automated follow-ups.

3. **Rebalancing Across Teams**

   o Redistribute cases among regions or teams where executives have spare capacity.

   o Use internal performance data to identify underutilized executives or teams.

4. **Field Resource Optimization**

   o **Cluster-Based Allocation:** Consolidate cases within geographic clusters to reduce travel time and increase efficiency.

   o **Centralized Handling for Low-Risk Accounts:** Assign a centralized team to handle low-risk cases, freeing field executives to focus on critical cases.

5. **Early Delinquency Control**

   o Strengthen collections in the X Bucket to minimize rollovers into higher buckets.

   o Conduct regular reviews of X Bucket strategies to pre-emptively address potential rollovers.

6. **Performance-Linked Allocation**

   o   Temporarily increase the ACR for high-performing executives during surges, with incentives for managing higher volumes.

   o   Closely monitor their productivity to avoid burnout or quality dips.

Maintaining the right ACR is crucial for sustaining collections performance and productivity. A sudden influx of cases can disrupt this balance, but with a well-thought-out contingency plan, banks and NBFCs can manage such situations effectively. Proactive measures such as workforce flexibility, technology integration, and early delinquency control ensure that the ACR remains within optimal levels, enabling smooth operations even during periods of stress.

07

Allocation Automation for Effective Collections

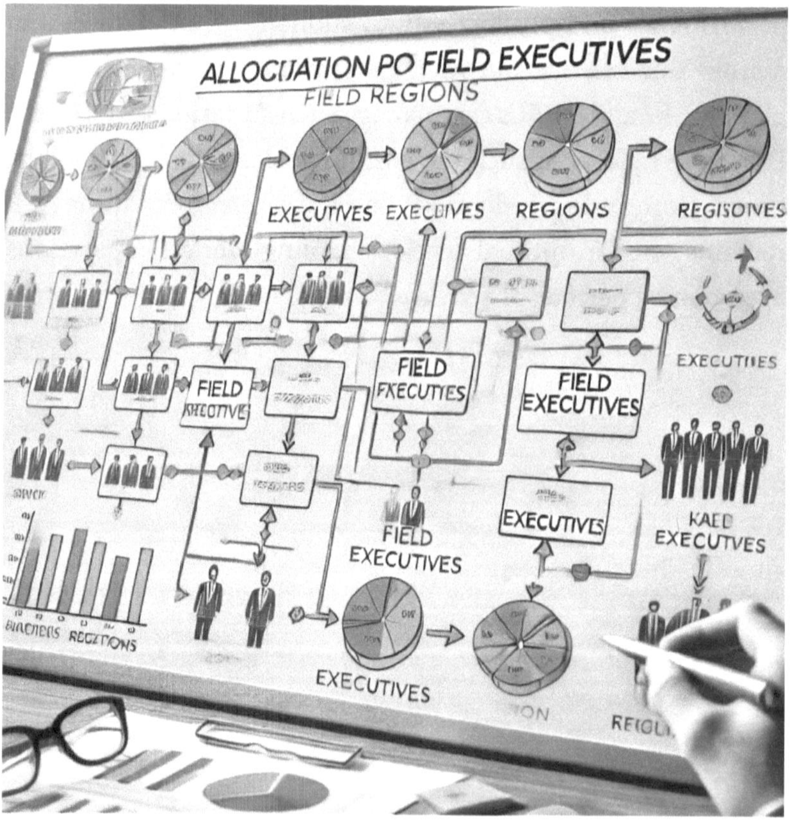

Automating the allocation process is a critical step toward transforming collections from a manual, time-intensive activity into a streamlined, data-driven operation.

By leveraging technology, banks and NBFCs can ensure that allocation decisions are objective, scalable, and aligned with both customer behaviour and employee performance metrics.

Core Principles of Allocation Automation

1. **Customer-Centric Allocation:** Focus on the customer rather than individual accounts. Consolidate all loan products under a customer's profile to avoid multiple collectors handling the same customer.

2. **Behaviour-Driven Assignment:** Use predictive analytics to determine customer behaviour scores (risk levels) and assign cases accordingly.

3. **Employee Performance Integration:** Allocate cases based on the historical performance and competency of collectors.

4. **ACR Compliance:** Maintain optimal Account Coverage Ratios (ACRs) to ensure balanced workloads and sustained productivity.

7.1 Technical Solution for Automated Allocation

Key Components of the Solution

1. **Centralized Data Repository (CDR):**
   - A unified database integrating:
     - Customer demographics, repayment history, and loan details.
     - Bureau data for external repayment behaviour.

- Employee performance metrics.

- Enables real-time access to data for allocation algorithms.

2. **Behaviour Scoring Engine:**

   o Generates customer-level risk scores by analysing:

   - Payment history (internal data).

   - Bureau data for market behaviour.

   - Geographical delinquency trends.

   - Product-specific performance in the portfolio.

   o Outputs a segmented risk score:

   - **VH (Very High Risk)**

   - **H (High Risk)**

   - **M (Medium Risk)**

   - **L (Low Risk)**

   - **VL (Very Low Risk)**

3. **Employee Performance Management System (EPMS):**

   o Evaluates collectors on:

   - Historical resolution rates (rollback and normalization).

   - Average daily customer visits.

   - Success rates in early vs. late-stage delinquency cases.

   - Customer handling feedback (if applicable).

- o Categorizes employees as:
    - **E (Excellent)**
    - **S (Satisfactory)**
    - **A (Average Performer)**
    - **U (Under Performer)**

4. **Allocation Logic Engine:**

- o The core automation system that:
    - Matches customer behaviour scores with employee ratings.
    - Considers geographical constraints and collector area familiarity.
    - Ensures compliance with predefined ACR thresholds.

- o Logic Example:
    - **VH Customers → E Collectors**, ACR ≤ 50 accounts.
    - **H Customers → S Collectors**, ACR ≤ 70 accounts.
    - **M Customers →** Mix of **S** and **A Collectors**, ACR ≤ 80 accounts.

5. **Real-Time Adjustment Module:**

- o Dynamically reallocates cases in response to:
    - Sudden inflow of cases (e.g., higher bucket rollovers).
    - Changes in collector availability or performance.
    - Customer behaviour changes (e.g., payment made).

6. **Dashboard and Analytics:**

   o A user-friendly interface for collections managers to:

     ▪ Monitor allocations and collector performance.

     ▪ Adjust allocation rules and thresholds as needed.

     ▪ Generate reports on portfolio segmentation, resolution rates, and more.

7.2 Framework and System Flow

Step 1: Data Ingestion

- Input data from internal systems (loan management system, CRM, HR performance data) and external sources (bureau reports, geographical trends).

- Consolidate data in the Centralized Data Repository.

Step 2: Customer Risk Scoring

- Behaviour Scoring Engine processes:

  o Repayment history and DPD trends.

  o Cross-product portfolio performance.

  o Market repayment behaviour from bureau data.

  o Generates a risk score for each customer.

Step 3: Employee Performance Scoring

- EPMS evaluates collectors and assigns performance ratings.

- Performance data is updated in real time based on daily activities.

Step 4: Allocation Logic Execution

- Allocation Logic Engine matches customer risk scores with collector ratings.

- Rules include:

  - Customer-Level Allocation: Consolidate all accounts under one customer profile.

  - ACR Compliance: Ensure collector workloads stay within predefined thresholds.

Step 5: Dynamic Adjustment

- Monitor portfolio changes (e.g., new delinquencies, rollbacks) and adjust allocations in real time.

- Reallocate accounts if collectors become unavailable or underperform.

Step 6: Monitoring and Feedback

- Use dashboards to track:

  - Collector productivity and resolution rates.

  - Portfolio-level recovery trends.

- Continuously refine allocation rules based on outcomes.

System Flow Diagram

Below is a conceptual flow for automation:

1. **Input Data Sources:**

   - Customer Data → Scoring Engine → Customer Risk Score.

   - Employee Data → EPMS → Employee Performance Score.

2. **Logic Engine Processing:**

   o   Inputs: Risk Score + Performance Score + ACR Rules.

   o   Outputs: Allocation Plan.

3. **Execution and Monitoring:**

   o   Allocation sent to collectors.

   o   Dashboards track execution and outcomes.

Benefits of Automated Allocation

1. **Efficiency Gains:**

   o   Eliminates manual allocation, saving time and reducing errors.

2. **Performance Optimization:**

   o   Matches high-risk cases with top-performing collectors, maximizing recovery potential.

3. **Dynamic Responsiveness:**

   o   Adjusts to real-time changes in portfolio and workforce conditions.

4. **Scalability:**

   o   Handles large portfolios with diverse customer profiles seamlessly.

5. **Enhanced Portfolio Quality:**

   o   Minimizes delinquency rollovers and ensures focused recovery efforts.

Automating the allocation process is not just about efficiency; it is about driving smarter decisions that enhance portfolio quality. By integrating customer behaviour scoring, employee performance metrics, and ACR compliance into a unified framework, banks and NBFCs can achieve sustainable improvements in their collections strategy. The next chapter will delve deeper into the customer behaviour scoring model, which forms the foundation of this automation process.

Collections Strategy

"The best strategy is the one that adapts."

- **Attributed to:** Charles Darwin's principle.

- **Background:** In collections, this highlights the importance of flexible strategies that evolve based on customer behaviour, economic shifts, and technological advancements.

08

A Deep Dive into a Robust Collections Strategy Framework

A **Collections Strategy** is a holistic and multi-layered approach designed to recover overdue accounts, prevent portfolio deterioration, and ensure the financial sustainability of the bank. It integrates the pillars of **People, Process, and Technology** to create a dynamic and responsive mechanism that balances efficiency with empathy. The strategy is underpinned by data-driven insights, early-warning mechanisms, and customer-centric interventions, ensuring timely action while maintaining long-term customer relationships. Below is a detailed exploration of the key elements of a comprehensive collections strategy:

8.1 Strategic Objectives and Intent

The primary objectives of a collections strategy align with the bank's broader goals of risk mitigation and financial stability:

- **Reducing TAT (Turnaround Time)**: Speeding up the recovery process is critical to minimizing financial exposure. The strategy emphasizes automating routine tasks, streamlining workflows, and reducing manual dependencies to ensure quicker resolutions.

- **Enhancing Resolution Rates**: The strategy employs advanced analytics and segmentation to prioritize accounts effectively, ensuring that resources are deployed where they have the highest likelihood of success.

- **Minimizing Losses**: By proactively identifying and addressing delinquent accounts before they escalate, the strategy helps reduce the bank's non-performing assets (NPAs) and financial write-offs.

- **Improving Portfolio Quality**: Maintaining a healthy performing book is a key focus. The strategy ensures regular repayments from non-delinquent customers while addressing risks through targeted interventions.

8.2   Early Detection with Early Warning Triggers

Proactive risk management begins with **early identification of potential defaults**:

- **Data-Driven Monitoring**: The bank continuously monitors customer behaviour using parameters such as missed payments, high credit utilization, sudden account inactivity, or frequent disputes.

- **Behavioural Analytics**: Advanced analytics models use historical repayment trends, socio-economic data, and spending patterns to predict the likelihood of default, enabling pre-emptive action.

- **Timely Nudges**: Personalized reminders and nudges, such as SMS alerts, emails, or app notifications, are sent to customers exhibiting early signs of delinquency. For example, a reminder might highlight the importance of maintaining a good credit score or offer flexible repayment options.

- **Custom Risk Scoring**: Customers are ranked based on their likelihood of default, enabling focused action on high-risk accounts and reducing wasted effort on low-risk ones.

8.3   Tailored Interventions for Diverse Customers

Recognizing that each customer's financial situation is unique, the strategy prioritizes **customized solutions**:

- **Customer Segmentation**: Customers are categorized into segments such as "High Intent to Pay," "Financially Distressed," and "Unresponsive," allowing for specialized recovery approaches.

- **Diverse Remedial Actions**: Examples of tailored interventions include:

  - **High-Intent Customers**: Offering grace periods, small discounts for early repayment, or loan restructuring.

  - **Financially Distressed Customers**: Proposing long-term instalment plans or partial debt forgiveness.

  - **Unresponsive Customers**: Increasing outreach frequency or escalating cases to field agents or legal teams.

- **Personalized Communication**: Depending on customer behaviour, outreach may include SMS, Emails, Voice Bot, WhatsApp, In-person visits, or Legal notices. For tech-savvy customers, digital channels like apps or chatbots may be prioritized.

8.4 Allocation and Deployment of Resources

Proper allocation of resources is a cornerstone of efficient collections:

- **Customer-Level Allocation**: Instead of assigning cases at the account level, the strategy focuses on the **customer level**, where all accounts linked to a single customer are handled together. This eliminates redundancy, reduces customer frustration, and enhances recovery rates.

- **Dynamic Allocation Framework**:

  - **Customer Behaviour Scores**: Cases are assigned based on predicted repayment likelihood and risk scores.

  - **Collector Performance Metrics**: High-performing collectors are assigned to high-priority cases for maximum impact.

  - **Geographical Optimization**: Cases are allocated to collectors based on proximity, reducing travel time and costs.

- **Account Coverage Ratio (ACR)**: Maintaining the right ACR ensures optimal workload distribution.

  - **For X Bucket Cases**: The ideal ACR is 70-80 accounts per collector.

  - **For 30+ DPD Cases**: The ratio drops to 50 accounts per collector to allow more intensive follow-ups.

  - **Contingency Plans**: A buffer team or external agency engagement ensures smooth operations during sudden case flow spikes.

8.5   Technology Integration

Technology acts as an enabler, making collections faster, smarter, and more cost-effective:

- **Automation**: Tasks such as sending payment reminders, generating defaulter reports, and escalating unresolved cases are automated to save time and reduce errors.

- **AI and Machine Learning**: Predictive algorithms help identify at-risk customers, recommend optimal communication channels, and forecast collection outcomes.

- **Digital Platforms**:

  - **Self-Service Portals**: Allow customers to make payments, request extensions, or update contact details without direct collector involvement.

  - **Mobile Apps for Field Agents**: Provide real-time updates, payment histories, and route optimization for field executives.

- ○ **Real-Time Dashboards**: Management can monitor recovery progress, collector performance, and portfolio health instantly.

- **Omnichannel Communication**: Integrated systems ensure seamless communication across SMS, emails, WhatsApp, IVR, and app notifications.

8.6 Process Optimization and Escalation Management

Streamlined processes ensure efficiency and transparency:

- **Standardized Operating Procedures (SOPs)**: Well-documented SOPs define the end-to-end collections lifecycle, ensuring consistency in approach.

- **Proactive Escalation Triggers**:

  - ○ **Legal Action**: Triggered for accounts with high outstanding amounts or repeated defaults.

  - ○ **External Recovery Agencies**: Deployed for geographically remote or highly unresponsive customers.

  - ○ **Settlement Approvals**: Automated thresholds determine which cases qualify for settlements, reducing decision delays.

- **Feedback Mechanisms**: Continuous input from field agents and supervisors is used to refine processes and improve efficiency.

8.7   Customer-Centric Approach

Empathy and customer engagement are at the heart of sustainable collections:

- **Empathetic Training for Field Agents**: Collectors are trained to handle sensitive situations, such as addressing financial distress, with patience and professionalism.

- **Flexibility in Repayment Plans**: Offering payment plans tailored to customer needs (e.g., deferred payments, reduced EMIs) helps maintain goodwill.

- **Transparent Communication**: Regular updates about outstanding amounts, payment options, and consequencesofnon-paymentreducemisunderstandings and increase customer trust.

8.8   Continuous Improvement

An effective collections strategy is never static; it evolves through learning and adaptation:

- **Data-Driven Insights**: Historical collections data is analysed to identify patterns, bottlenecks, and areas for improvement.

- **Regulatory Adaptations**: Compliance with changing laws, such as those governing fair debt collection practices, ensures ethical operations.

- **Ongoing Training**: Collectors are continuously trained on new tools, negotiation techniques, and customer engagement strategies.

- **Performance Monitoring**: Regular reviews of key metrics like recovery rates, TAT, and ACR help assess and refine the strategy.

8.9   Cost and Efficiency Optimization

Balancing the cost-to-collect ratio is crucial for sustainable operations:

- **Digital First, Field Later**: Prioritize low-cost digital channels for initial outreach and reserve field visits for high-value or critical cases.

- **Automated Cost Analysis**: Tools track recovery costs relative to outstanding amounts, ensuring efforts remain economically viable.

A bank's collections strategy is a sophisticated framework that combines people, process, and technology to address delinquency at every stage of the recovery lifecycle. By leveraging early-warning triggers, tailored interventions, optimized resource allocation, and advanced technology, the strategy ensures a balance between operational efficiency and customer-centricity. Continuous improvement, coupled with a clear focus on empathy and transparency, makes the strategy adaptable to evolving challenges and critical for sustaining portfolio quality and financial stability.

Strategic Execution for Core Collections

"A stitch in time saves nine."

- This proverb reflects the importance of acting promptly to prevent larger issues. In collections, it signifies the value of pre-delinquency management and early intervention strategies.

09

Pre-Delinquency Management (PDM)

What is PDM?

Pre-Delinquency Management involves engaging with customers before they miss their payments. The focus is on timely reminders and support, ensuring regular payments and avoiding delinquencies.

9.1 Benefits of Pre-Delinquency Management (PDM)

1. Proactively Reduces Delinquencies: PDM's proactive approach significantly reduces delinquencies by addressing potential payment issues before they evolve into full-fledged defaults. Early engagement through targeted reminders and nudges ensures that customers are consistently reminded of their payment obligations. By identifying and intervening with high-risk customers early, even before they miss a payment, PDM prevents the escalation of delinquencies into higher-risk stages that would typically require more aggressive recovery actions. This early intervention is key to minimizing the number of accounts that enter the delinquency pipeline, thus lowering the overall delinquency rates across the portfolio. The proactive nature of PDM fosters financial discipline among customers, reducing the likelihood of overdue payments and avoiding the need for extensive recovery procedures down the line.

2. Strengthens Customer Relationships: PDM doesn't just focus on collecting payments; it focuses on creating positive, ongoing relationships with customers. By engaging with customers before they miss a payment, PDM demonstrates the institution's commitment to their financial well-being. Through timely, personalized communication, customers feel supported, not pressured, which builds trust. This nurturing approach fosters customer loyalty and increases the likelihood of future business engagements. Additionally, PDM often includes flexibility in payment options, which can further strengthen the relationship, as customers appreciate institutions that show empathy toward their financial challenges. By resolving queries promptly and addressing customer concerns, banks and NBFCs can enhance customer satisfaction, creating a sense of partnership rather than one-sided transactional engagement. Stronger relationships translate into higher retention rates and greater customer lifetime value, benefiting both the customer and the institution.

3. Lowers Operational Costs Associated with Recovery Processes: A well-implemented PDM strategy can significantly lower the operational costs associated with recovery efforts. By preventing accounts from falling into delinquency or becoming severely overdue, PDM reduces the need for costly and resource-intensive recovery actions, such as phone calls from agents, field visits, or legal proceedings. Early intervention through automated reminders and nudges reduces the workload on collections teams, freeing them up to focus on more complex or high-priority cases. Moreover, PDM leverages automation through tools like voice bots, SMS, WhatsApp, and other messaging platforms, which can engage thousands of customers at once, minimizing manual effort. This level of automation lowers labour costs, enhances process efficiency, and ensures a consistent approach to customer engagement. As the need for intensive manual follow-up is reduced, the bank or NBFC can allocate resources more effectively, leading to a leaner, more cost-efficient collections process.

4. Improves Overall Portfolio Quality: By addressing payment issues before they escalate, PDM significantly improves the overall quality of the portfolio. The proactive nature of PDM helps maintain accounts in good standing, reducing the incidence of non-performing assets (NPAs) and improving the overall health of the loan book. The early identification and engagement with high-risk customers prevent them from progressing into more severe delinquency stages, thereby keeping the accounts current and minimizing potential write-offs. Additionally, PDM's segmentation-based approach enables tailored communications for different customer risk profiles, ensuring that each customer receives the right type of engagement, which enhances the effectiveness of the strategy. As customers remain aware of their obligations and are encouraged to pay on time, the bank's or NBFC's portfolio becomes more stable, with fewer accounts at risk of default. This improved portfolio quality leads to enhanced credit ratings, better financial performance, and greater investor confidence in the institution's operations. Furthermore, by automating and scaling PDM, institutions can efficiently manage a larger volume of customers, ensuring that personalized engagement is maintained even as the customer base grows.

Summary: The benefits of Pre-Delinquency Management (PDM) are substantial, ranging from a proactive reduction in delinquencies and operational cost savings to strengthening customer relationships and improving portfolio quality. By engaging with customers early, addressing payment concerns before they become problems, and leveraging automation, PDM helps create a healthier financial environment for both customers and institutions. The ability to resolve issues early, combined with a customer-centric approach, not only reduces costs but also fosters trust and loyalty, resulting in long-term success for the institution and its clients.

Strategies in PDM

1. **Nudging Strategies:** Nudging is the cornerstone of PDM, involving systematic reminders and engagements with customers.

Segmentation-Based Nudging:

Customer Risk Category	Mode of Communication	Frequency	Message Tone
Very High / High Risk	Voice Bot + SMS/ WhatsApp	T - 8, T - 3	Urgent, personalized support
Medium Risk	Voice Bot + SMS/ WhatsApp	T - 3	Friendly reminder
Low / Very Low Risk	SMS/WhatsApp	T - 3	General notification

Voice Bot Success:

- o **Scalability:** Capable of reaching millions of customers.

- o **Interactive:** Able to answer queries or escalate issues to human agents.

- o **Disposition Tracking:** Logs customer responses for further analysis and action.

2. **Behaviour-Based Communication**

- o High-risk customers receive personalized reminders emphasizing urgency.

- o Low-risk customers are engaged with light, non-intrusive reminders.

3. **Channel Diversification**

- o Voice Bots for immediate, real-time interaction.

- o SMS/WhatsApp for quick and cost-effective communication.

- o Emails for detailed and formal reminders.

4. **Automated Query Handling**

- o Voice bots or chatbots handle FAQs and escalate unresolved queries to human agents, analysis and resolve.

A detailed PDM Process:

Below is the indicative process flow of PDM calling process and Contact Strategy.

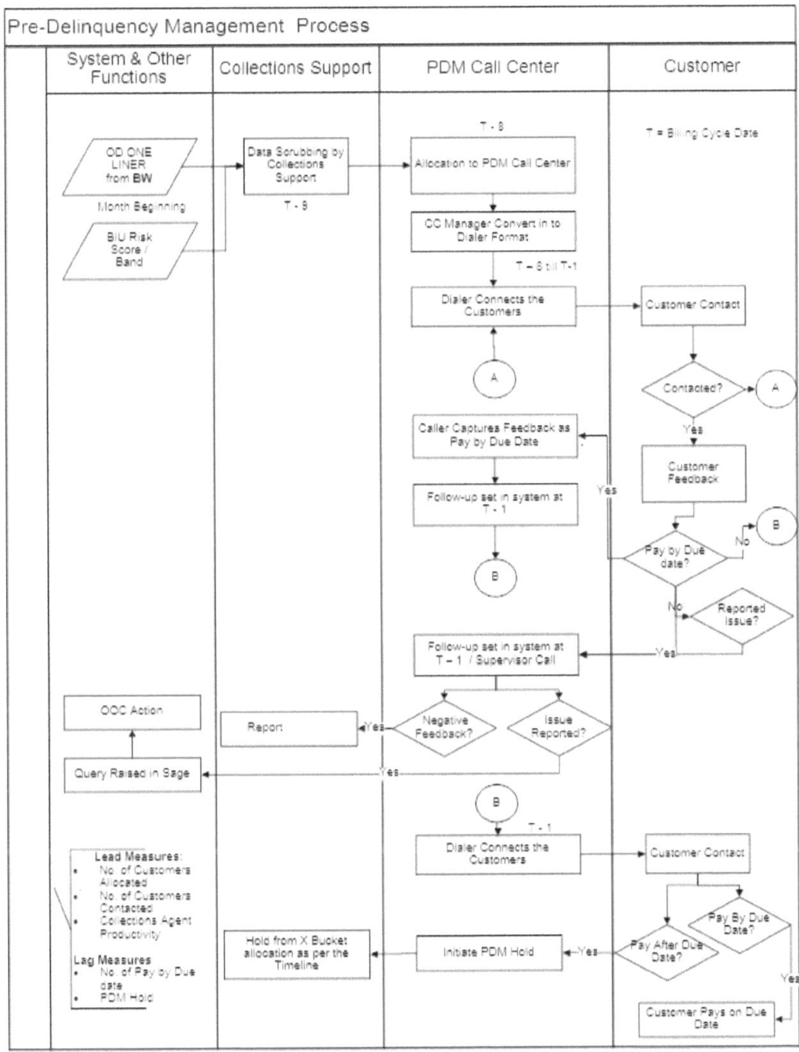

PDM is a critical component of the core collections process. By leveraging advanced technology, segmentation strategies, and empathetic communication, banks and NBFCs can proactively address potential defaults, enhance portfolio quality, and strengthen customer relationships.

The next chapter will explore **Early-Stage Delinquency Management (EDM)** and how a systematic escalation framework can further minimize risks and optimize collections outcomes.

"PDM is like unlocking the controlled release of a dam's floodgates, ensuring a steady minimal flow that keeps portfolio secure."

10

Bucket X Strategy

Comprehensive Step-by-Step Approach for Early Delinquency Management

Overview of Bucket X:

Bucket X represents the first stage of early delinquency in the collections process. It involves customers who fail to make their payment on time, but importantly, they are not in arrears from previous billing cycles. These customers may be habitual payers who encounter temporary financial difficulties, or they could represent more serious underlying issues that need careful handling.

The missed EMI in Bucket X is usually an isolated incident, often due to financial stress, personal emergencies, or a temporary setback. As such, it presents an opportunity for banks to intervene early and resolve the situation, preventing further delinquency. However, how the bank responds to this early-stage default is critical for managing customer relationships, ensuring timely payments, and maintaining portfolio quality.

10.1   Key Factors for Managing Bucket X

1. **Customer Segmentation**: Customers in Bucket X are typically divided into categories based on their payment behaviour and the reason for the missed EMI. Effective segmentation allows for personalized, targeted strategies.

   o **Regular Payers (Temporary Financial Stress)**: These customers have historically paid on time but missed a payment due to temporary financial stress (e.g., unexpected expenses or income disruption).

   o **Customers Rolled Back from Higher Buckets**: Customers who were previously in higher delinquency buckets (Bucket 1 or Bucket 2+) and returned to good standing but are now defaulting again.

   o **First EMI Bounce (High-Risk Trigger)**: A missed first EMI that may signal deeper financial issues and presents the highest risk.

2. **Proactive Communication**: Communication is key in Bucket X. Early intervention, timely reminders, and empathetic engagement can help resolve the situation quickly, especially when the customer is experiencing temporary financial challenges.

3. **Close Coordination Between Teams**: The call center and field collection teams need to work closely together to ensure information sharing, effective follow-ups, and seamless intervention.

10.2 Step-by-Step Approach for Managing Bucket X

Step 1: Early Identification and Segmentation

- **Within 24-48 hours of missed payment**, identify all customers who are now in Bucket X. These are customers who have bounced the current month's EMI but have no overdue payments from previous months.

- **Segmentation**: Segment the customers into categories based on their payment history:

  - **Category A**: Regular payers who missed an EMI due to temporary financial stress.

  - **Category B**: Customers rolled back from higher buckets and have bounced an EMI.

  - **Category C**: High-risk customers who missed their first EMI or have missed multiple payments despite a history of regular payments.

Step 2: Immediate Action for Category A (Regular Payers with Temporary Stress)

For customers who are habitual payers and are experiencing temporary financial distress:

- **Communication**: Reach out to the customer within 2-3 days of the missed payment. Use a **polite, empathetic tone** to inquire about the missed payment. Remind them of their strong payment history.

- **Empathy and Support**: Acknowledge that financial difficulties can happen and offer to help them resolve the issue. Some potential options include:

  - **Rescheduling the EMI**: Offer to move the due date to a later time or extend the tenure to reduce the EMI amount.

  - **Partial Payment Option**: Allow for partial payments if the customer cannot pay the full EMI but can pay a portion.

  - **Deferment Options**: If needed, offer a deferment for the current month's EMI and allow the customer to catch up in the subsequent months.

- **Technology**: Use **automated SMS/WhatsApp reminders** along with **voice bots** that send gentle reminders to the customer, followed by a phone call from a collections agent if necessary.

Step 3: Action for Category B (Customers Rolled Back from Higher Buckets)

Customers who have returned to good standing but are now defaulting require extra caution and attention:

- **Review Historical Payment Behaviour**: Analyse the customer's previous delinquencies and identify the reason they were moved from a higher bucket to normal. This will give insight into potential recurring financial issues.

- **Communication and Assessment**: Reach out to the customer immediately (within 2-3 days). **Conduct a thorough assessment** to understand if the missed

EMI is due to temporary cash flow problems or if it's a sign of deeper financial issues.

- **Flexible Payment Solutions**: Offer flexible solutions such as rescheduling, loan tenure extension, or offering a grace period.

- **Monitor Closely**: Increase follow-up frequency for these customers, as they have a higher likelihood of moving back into higher delinquency buckets if not managed carefully.

Step 4: High-Risk Cases – First EMI Bounce (Category C)

A missed first EMI is the highest risk in Bucket X and requires immediate, intensive intervention.

- **Immediate Response**: Contact the customer within **48 hours of missed payment**. Given the severity, try to speak directly to the customer, explaining the importance of regular payments, especially at the beginning of the loan.

- **Understand the Reason for Default**: It's critical to understand why the customer missed the first EMI. Was it due to an administrative issue, or does the customer have genuine financial difficulties?

- **Offer Solutions**:

  - **Restructure the Loan**: Offer flexible repayment plans such as extending the loan tenure or revising the EMI to make it more affordable.

  - **Financial Counselling**: If needed, offer financial counselling services or refer the customer to a financial advisor to help manage their expenses better.

- **Escalation**: If the customer's behaviour indicates a deeper financial problem, consider escalating the case to senior collections teams for further intervention.

Step 5: Allocate Accounts Based on Risk Profile and Collect Feedback

- **Allocation Process**:

    - **Call Center Allocation**: For initial contact, allocate Bucket X customers to the call center agents based on the risk segmentation. High-risk customers (Category C) should be prioritized.

    - **Field Collections Allocation**: If the call center fails to reach the customer, escalate the case to the field collections team for in-person visits.

    - **Follow-up Protocol**: Follow the standard protocol for daily/weekly allocation based on bounce entries. Monitor progress carefully and ensure agents are working within their **ACR (Account Coverage Ratio)** limits.

Step 6: Integration of Call Center and Field Teams

Close coordination between the call center and field teams is essential for the timely resolution of Bucket X cases.

- **Communication and Collaboration**:

    - Call center agents and field executives should be in **constant communication**. The call center team can share feedback from customers with the field team, while the field team can provide real-time information that can help call center agents refine their outreach approach.

- ○ **Joint Conference Calls**: For high-risk or unresponsive customers, arrange **conference calls** between call center agents and field executives to resolve the issue in a collaborative manner.

Step 7: Timely and Proactive Follow-Up

- **Timeliness**: Ensure that follow-up communication occurs within a well-defined window. For instance, **call center agents should attempt to contact customers within 3 days**, and if no contact is made, **field teams should step in on the 4th day**. The field team should aim to visit customers within 5 days.

- **Automated Updates**: Use automated systems to track customer responses and update the dialler with new contact information if necessary. This ensures no follow-up is missed.

Step 8: Offer Resolution and Retain Customer Credibility

- **Resolution and Payment Regularization**: Focus on resolving the missed payment issue as quickly as possible. Offer solutions that will help the customer return to regular payments without further penalties or negative impacts on their credit score.

- **Maintaining Customer Dignity**: Treat each customer with respect and dignity. Do not create an adversarial relationship, as this can damage the customer's financial credibility. Instead, help them re-establish their payment habits with empathy and understanding.

- **Transparency and Education**: Educate customers about the impact of late payments on their credit history and provide clear guidance on how they can avoid future issues. This not only helps resolve the immediate issue but also promotes financial literacy and prevents future defaults.

Monitoring and Reporting

- **Daily Monitoring**: Closely track all cases in Bucket X, ensuring that no customer is left unaddressed. Regular reports should be generated to monitor the effectiveness of the outreach efforts and ensure customers are being followed up on time.

- **Feedback Loop**: Ensure continuous feedback from both the call center and field teams. Analyse the data to refine the strategy and make necessary adjustments to the approach.

The Bucket X strategy is a crucial part of early delinquency management. By carefully managing customers who miss a payment in this early stage, banks can ensure that these defaults do not escalate into more severe delinquencies. Using a tailored, empathetic, and proactive approach, backed by close coordination between the call center and field teams, banks can manage these cases effectively, maintain customer relationships, and enhance portfolio quality. With timely intervention and personalized solutions, Bucket X can serve as an opportunity for the bank to demonstrate its commitment to customers' financial well-being, fostering long-term trust and loyalty.

A Critical Transition: Proactive Engagement in Bucket X to Prevent Delinquency.

10.3   Bucket X: Calling Strategy

The below is just the indicative X Bucket Strategic process. You can replace the call centre with Voice Bot here or both can co-exist.

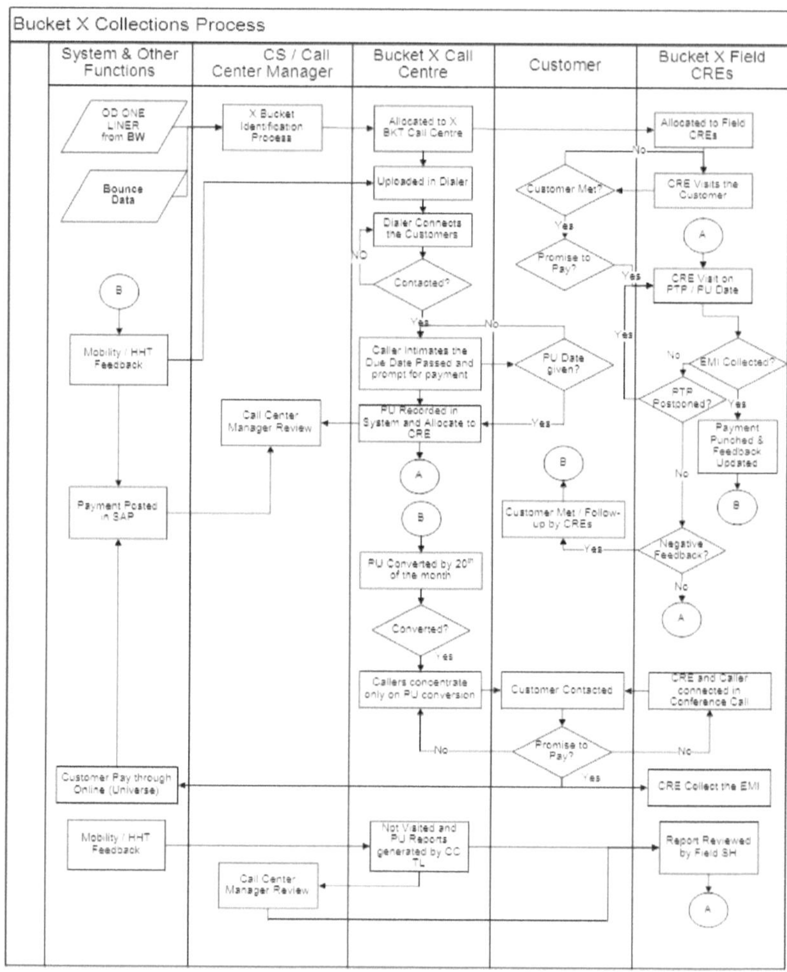

The Role of Voice and Chatbots in Bucket X

The inclusion of Voice Bots and Chatbots in Bucket X collections is a game-changer, enhancing the efficiency, reach, and effectiveness of the collections process. Here's a detailed overview of the benefits and reasons for their integration:

1. **Humanized Automation with GenAI Technology**

   - Voice bots powered by GenAI replicate human interactions, making communication feel personalized and empathetic.

   - This humanized touch fosters trust and ensured that customers feel valued, not pressured, even when dealing with sensitive financial matters.

2. **Instant Outreach Post-Bounce**

   - Speed is critical in Bucket X collections, where immediate engagement with customers post-bounce can prevent delinquency escalation.

   - Voice bots can contact thousands of customers instantly, ensuring timely communication that a call center might delay due to limited bandwidth.

3. **Scalable Engagement**

   - Voice bots and chatbots handle a large volume of interactions simultaneously, enabling banks to cover their entire portfolio without strain.

   - This scalability ensures no customer is left unattended, maintaining high service levels across all segments.

4. **Efficient Query Handling**

   - Automated bots can address a wide range of customer queries, including payment instructions, account details, or EMI schedules.

- By resolving simple to moderately complex issues on the spot, bots reduce dependency on human agents and improve first-contact resolution rates.

5. **Seamless Escalation to Human Agents**

   - For more complex issues that require human intervention, bots seamlessly transfer the interaction to a live agent.

   - This ensures that no customer query goes unresolved while maintaining operational efficiency.

6. **Integrated Payment Journey**

   - Voice bots can integrate with real-time payment systems, allowing customers to make payments directly during the call.

   - Chatbots on platforms like WhatsApp can share secure payment links, simplifying the payment process and reducing friction.

7. **Cost Efficiency**

   - By automating initial customer engagement and query resolution, bots significantly reduce the operational costs of running call centres.

   - With bots managing at least 50% of customer interactions, banks can allocate human resources more effectively to high-priority cases.

8. **Personalized Customer Engagement**

    o   Bots adapt communication based on customer profiles, ensuring that interactions are relevant and tailored.

    o   High-risk customers receive urgent, supportive messaging, while low-risk customers are engaged with friendly reminders.

9. **24/7 Availability**

    o   Voice bots and chatbots operate round the clock, ensuring customers can reach out at their convenience, regardless of time zones or working hours.

    o   This continuous availability enhances customer satisfaction and increases the likelihood of timely resolutions.

10. **Data-Driven Insights**

    o   Bots collect valuable interaction data, such as customer feedback, response times, and behavioural patterns.

    o   This data can be analysed to refine communication strategies, predict repayment behaviour, and optimize resource allocation.

11. **Multichannel Integration**

    o   Voice bots complement chatbots across platforms like WhatsApp, SMS, and email, offering customers multiple channels to engage.

    o   This omnichannel approach caters to diverse customer preferences, improving reach and effectiveness.

12. **Faster Resolution and Higher Recovery Rates**

    o The speed and efficiency of bots in reaching customers immediately post-bounce ensure faster resolutions, reducing the chances of accounts slipping into delinquency.

    o Early engagement and timely follow-ups improve overall recovery rates.

13. **Customer-Centric Approach**

    o Bots offer an empathetic, non-intrusive method of communication, ensuring customers do not feel harassed.

    o By providing solutions promptly and addressing concerns with care, bots enhance the customer experience, preserving their dignity and trust.

14. **Operational Streamlining**

    o By handling repetitive tasks such as sending reminders or providing account information, bots free up human agents to focus on complex cases.

    o This targeted approach ensures efficient use of resources and improved overall productivity.

15. **Proactive Nurturing of Customer Relationships**

    o Regular and personalized interactions through bots ensure customers remain engaged and aware of their payment obligations.

o   This proactive approach strengthens customer relationships, fostering loyalty and long-term engagement.

16. **Language and Regional Flexibility**

o   Advanced bots can communicate in multiple languages and dialects, catering to diverse customer bases.

o   This inclusivity ensures that communication barriers do not hinder engagement.

17. **Reduced Risk of Delinquency Escalation**

o   The speed, personalization, and efficiency of bot-driven communication help mitigate the risk of accounts transitioning into higher delinquency buckets.

o   Early identification of customer concerns through bot interactions enables banks to take pre-emptive action.

Incorporating Voice Bots and Chatbots in Bucket X collections transforms the process into a highly efficient, customer-friendly, and cost-effective operation. The ability to scale, personalize, and streamline interactions ensures timely resolutions while preserving customer dignity. With technology enabling a seamless payment journey and reducing operational burdens, banks can achieve higher recovery rates and build stronger customer relationships, ultimately enhancing portfolio quality and financial performance.

11

Early Delinquency Collections Strategy

A Comprehensive Approach for Managing 30–90 DPD Customers

Managing early delinquency collections, particularly for customers who have missed payments beyond their next billing cycle (30–90 DPD), is one of the most critical tasks for banks and financial institutions. These cases require not only a well-structured strategy to reduce the risks associated with overdue loans but also an empathetic approach to maintain strong customer relationships. The goal is to minimize delinquencies, protect customer creditworthiness, and ensure the bank's financial health. Below is a detailed step-by-step approach for managing early delinquency collections effectively.

11.1 Importance of Early Delinquency Collections

1. **Protecting Customer Creditworthiness**

   - **Impact on Credit Score:** Customers who miss payments beyond the due date and fall into early delinquency (30-90 DPD) risk damaging their credit scores. A low credit score severely affects their future borrowing ability and can also increase their cost of borrowing.

- **Bank's Responsibility:** It's the bank's responsibility to help customers understand the consequences of delayed payments and to assist them in rectifying the situation before their credit health is irreparably harmed. Educating customers on the importance of timely payments can prevent their financial reputation from being adversely affected.

2. **Preventing Escalation to Higher Buckets**

- **Risk of Further Delinquencies:** Accounts that reach 30+ DPD and are not addressed promptly often slip into higher buckets (e.g., 60 DPD, 90 DPD), where the risk of becoming a non-performing asset (NPA) is much higher. Higher buckets also carry increased operational costs, as they require more intensive collection efforts and legal interventions.

- **Cost of Recovery:** Proactive engagement at this stage can prevent costly recovery actions, reduce the potential of future write-offs, and improve the overall portfolio performance.

3. **Enhancing Portfolio Quality**

- **Minimizing GNPA:** Addressing early delinquencies ensures that the accounts are regularized before they escalate. This reduces the Gross Non-Performing Asset (GNPA) ratio and the likelihood of high loan defaults.

- **Regulatory Compliance:** By regularizing early delinquencies, the bank ensures compliance with regulatory guidelines, avoiding penalties related to asset quality and provisioning requirements.

4. **Strengthening Customer Relationships**

- **Customer Retention:** A well-managed early delinquency collection process helps build trust and strengthens customer relationships. By helping and showing empathy, customers are more likely to stay loyal to the bank and continue their relationship, improving customer retention in the long term.

- **Positive Brand Image:** A bank that handles early delinquency with understanding, flexibility, and prompt action earns a positive reputation for customer-centricity, which can drive brand loyalty and lead to more referrals.

11.2   Tracking Mechanisms for Early Delinquency

1. **Centralized Dashboards**

- **Real-Time Monitoring:** Use centralized dashboards to track key metrics such as the number of delinquent accounts, resolution rates, overdue amounts, and recovery percentages. These dashboards can be configured to display data in real time, giving managers a holistic view of collections performance.

- **Visualization of Data:** These dashboards should allow data to be visualized across various dimensions—by geography, branch, customer segments, etc. This enables better tracking of early delinquencies and quick identification of problem areas.

2. **Portfolio Prioritization**

- **Risk Segmentation:** Segment the portfolio based on the risk level and historical behaviour of the customer. For instance, customers who have missed payments for the first time may be categorized differently from habitual defaulters. This ensures targeted strategies and allows for more personalized approaches.

- **Priority Setting:** High-risk accounts should be prioritized for faster resolution. With limited resources, segmenting customers by risk levels ensures that collection efforts are focused where they are needed the most.

3. **Geo-Tagging Field Visits**

- **Field Visit Management:** Use geo-tagging technology to ensure that field executives visit the correct locations and that visits are tracked for transparency. Geo-tagging helps managers track the field executive's location in real time, verifying that they are completing assigned visits and addressing the correct customers.

- **Real-Time Reporting:** Field agents can report back immediately after a visit, capturing data on the customer's situation and the outcome of the meeting, ensuring that the data is up-to-date and accessible to supervisors for further action.

4. **Automation and Alerts**

- **Automated Alerts:** Set up automated alerts to notify the collections team about approaching due dates, missed payments, or overdue accounts. These alerts should be actionable, prompting collections agents to take the necessary steps to engage the customer before the situation worsens.

- **Escalation Alerts:** Automated escalation alerts help notify managers when accounts are at risk of becoming high-risk, enabling prompt intervention.

5. **Comprehensive Performance Metrics**

- **KPIs and Metrics:** Track performance using key performance indicators (KPIs) like call and visit volumes, resolution rates, customer satisfaction scores, and average time to resolution. Regularly monitoring these metrics helps supervisors gauge the effectiveness of the collections process.

- **Trend Analysis:** Use trend analysis to identify potential issues early on and adapt the strategy to improve outcomes. For example, if certain regions or customer segments consistently perform poorly, these areas can be given extra attention.

11.3   Early Bucket Field Strategy Flow

The below mentioned flow is just the indictive flow for an Asset Collections flow. This can be used as guiding principle to set up the banks early bucket allocation till resolution.

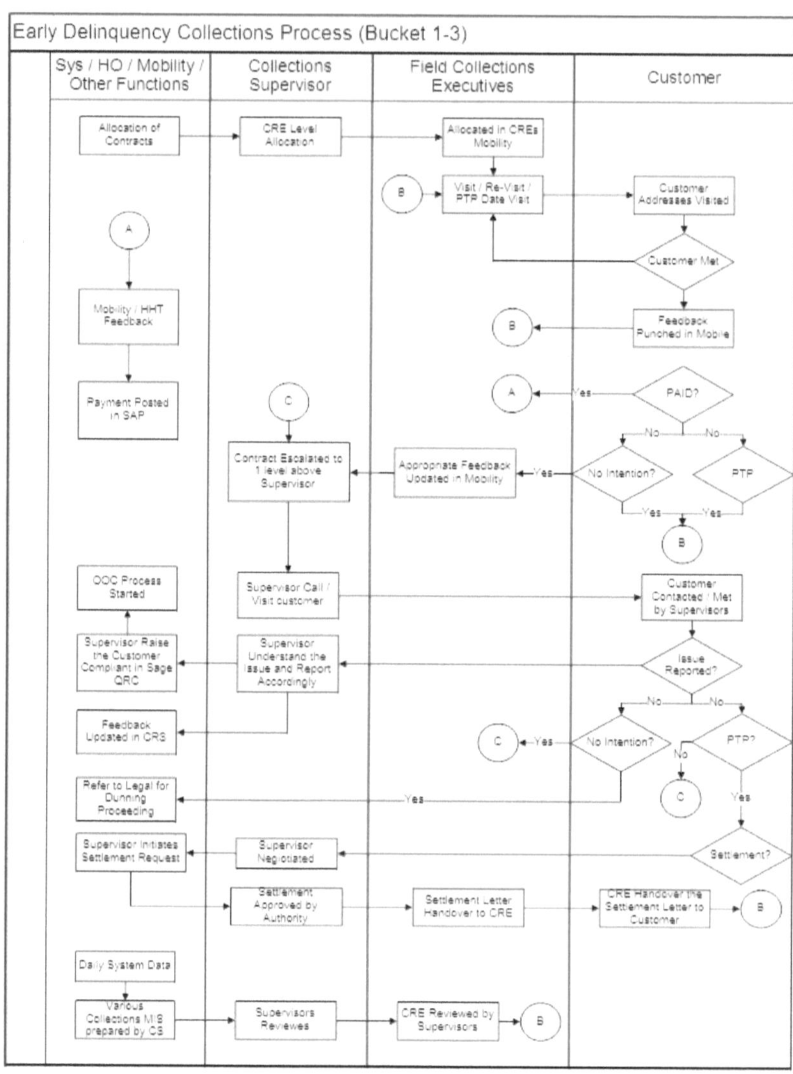

11.4   Communication Strategies

1.   Educating Customers

- **Financial Literacy:** Use communication as an opportunity to educate customers about the consequences of non-payment and the importance of maintaining a good credit score. Offering tools and resources for financial management (e.g., budgeting tips, repayment calculators) can help customers better manage their finances.

- **Transparent Communication:** Clearly explain the payment options available to customers and the impact of continued non-payment. This transparency helps manage customer expectations and builds trust.

2. **Regular and Proactive Nudges**

- **Multiple Communication Channels:** Use a variety of communication channels, such as SMS, emails, automated voice messages, and WhatsApp notifications to reach customers. Early communication helps set the tone and urgency for the situation.

- **Personalized Reminders:** Customize reminders based on the customer's profile and situation. A personalized approach increases the chances of the customer responding and resolving the issue before it escalates.

3. **Tailored Messaging**

- **First-Time Defaulters:** Send empathetic messages explaining the importance of regularizing their payment and offering flexible solutions (e.g., repayment plans, rescheduling). Provide educational material to help them understand how late payments could affect their credit.

- **RepeatDefaulters:**Adoptafirmertone,emphasizing the risk of escalating consequences. However, continue to offer solutions, like restructuring or legal support, to resolve the delinquency.

4. **Field-Driven Engagement**

- **Personalized Field Engagement:** Field staff should meet customers in person to discuss the situation and work together to find a resolution. This face-to-face engagement builds rapport and can be more effective in addressing complex issues.

- **Follow-Up Calls and Visits:** Follow-up calls should complement field visits, ensuring consistent communication and reinforcing the message to the customer.

5. **Two-Way Communication**

- **Empowering Customers:** Allow customers to raise concerns, request alternate payment options, and negotiate terms. A two-way communication model makes customers feel heard and valued, enhancing their willingness to cooperate.

11.5 Field Collection Strategies

1. **Empathetic Approach**

- **Active Listening:** Field agents must listen actively to the customer's issues, whether financial difficulties or personal challenges, and respond empathetically. This understanding can open opportunities for customers to seek assistance and work out payment solutions.

- **Non-Confrontational Communication**: Avoid confrontational language and instead focus on solutions and shared goals. Customers are more likely to cooperate when they feel supported.

2. **Strategic Visit Plans**

- **Prioritizing High-Risk Accounts**: Ensure that visits are scheduled for high-risk accounts, particularly those that show signs of potential escalation to higher DPD buckets.

- **Balancing Urban and Rural Areas**: Adjust the field agent's visit schedule based on customer density and geographic reach. In rural areas, where visits may take longer, agents must be provided with adequate support and resources.

3. **Physical Presence**

- **In-Person Meetings:** A visit from a field agent communicates the seriousness of the situation and serves as a reminder of the bank's commitment to resolving the issue. This in-person contact also helps the agent understand the customer's circumstances more clearly.

- **Evidence Collection:** Field staff can also collect evidence of the customer's situation, which can be important for determining the appropriate next steps, including legal escalation if needed.

4. **Collaborative Efforts**

   - **Collaboration with Call Centres:** The field team should work closely with the call center team to ensure consistency in communication and messaging. Sharing customer feedback and visit outcomes between teams ensures that the customer is not bombarded with conflicting messages.

   - **Real-Time Information Sharing:** Use mobile apps or platforms where field staff can update the progress of their visits, share customer feedback, and escalate unresolved issues for quick resolution.

5. **Differentiated Treatment**

   - **Approach for First-Time Defaulters:** For customers with a one-time delay, offer flexible repayment options like extensions or adjusted schedules.

   - **Approach for Habitual Defaulters:** For repeat offenders, adopt more structured approaches, including discussions about stricter consequences, and explore legal avenues for enforcement if needed.

11.6 Managing Intentional Defaulters

1. **Behavioural Analysis**

   - **Defaulter Profiling:** Regularly analyse customers' payment history to determine patterns of intentional non-payment. Use this analysis to craft personalized approaches.

- **Warning Signs:** Identify warning signs of intentional defaults, such as frequent partial payments, refusal to answer calls, or inconsistent excuses.

2. **Legal Escalations**

   - **Leveraging Legal Tools:** Use tools such as:

     - **Section 138 of the Negotiable Instruments Act** for cheque bounce cases.

     - **SARFAESI Act** for secured loans.

     - **Lok Adalat** for amicable dispute resolutions.

   - **Escalation Process:** Clearly outline the steps for escalation to legal authorities and ensure that the process is transparent, minimizing the chances of litigation while maximizing the chances of timely resolution.

3. **Highlighting Consequences**

   - **Emphasizing the Legal Ramifications:** Make customers aware of the legal implications, including the risk of court proceedings and the negative impact on their creditworthiness.

   - **Firm yet Fair Communication:** While the approach should remain firm, emphasize that the goal is to work with the customer to find a solution, with legal action being a last resort.

11.7   Supervisor's Role in Managing Field Staff

1. **Regular Performance Reviews**

   - **Daily and Weekly Reviews:** Supervisors should conduct regular performance reviews to assess field staff productivity and effectiveness in addressing delinquent accounts. These reviews should focus on visit completion rates, successful resolutions, and customer engagement levels.

   - **KPIs and Metrics:** Review key performance indicators (KPIs) such as successful payment recovery rates, customer satisfaction scores, and field visits completed against targets.

2. **Real-Time Feedback**

   - **Instant Reporting and Feedback:** Supervisors should leverage technology (mobile apps, online dashboards) to provide real-time feedback to field agents after every visit. This can help correct issues immediately and provide guidance for future interactions.

3. **Nudging and Coaching**

   - **Motivational Nudges:** Regular nudges, both positive and constructive, keep the staff motivated and focused on their targets. Supervisors should act as coaches, helping agents improve their customer handling and negotiation skills.

- **Coaching on Difficult Situations:** Train field staff on how to deal with tough customers, handle objections, and close conversations effectively without confrontation.

4. **Resource Allocation**

- **Optimizing Staff Deployment:** Supervisors should monitor workload distribution to ensure that field agents are effectively allocated to high-priority, high-risk cases, and ensure no one is overburdened.

11.8 Target Setting to Minimize GNPA

1. **Realistic Targets**

- **Data-Driven Targets:** Set realistic targets based on historical data, adjusting them for the performance levels of individual field agents or regions. Targets should focus on minimizing GNPA, reducing the number of days overdue, and maximizing recoveries.

- **Incentivizing Results:** Incentive programs tied to resolution rates and target achievement encourage field staff to focus on high-priority delinquent accounts.

2. **Payment Preponement**

- **Encouraging Early Payments:** Promote early payments at the beginning of the month, rather than waiting until the end. This helps avoid the backlog of accounts and ensures that delinquency cases are addressed promptly.

3. **Incentive Mechanisms**

- **Incentives for High Performance:** Introduce incentive mechanisms based on collections targets, customer satisfaction, and successful regularization rates. This motivates the field staff and encourages productive engagement with customers.

11.9   Techniques to Track Productivity

1. **Daily Activity Logs**

- **Detailed Logs:** Require field staff to maintain detailed logs of their daily activities, including customer visits, resolutions, follow-up actions, and any obstacles encountered. These logs provide transparency and offer data for performance evaluation.

2. **Geo-Tagged Reporting**

- **Verification of Visits:** Use geo-tagging technology to ensure that the field visits are happening at the right locations. This feature ensures that staff are adhering to schedules and improving accountability.

3. **Comparative Analysis**

- **Team Performance Analysis:** Perform comparative analysis of team performance to spot the best-performing agents and areas that require improvement. Sharing best practices and setting benchmarks can lead to a more consistent collection approach.

4. Digital Tools

- **AI-Powered Insights:** Utilize AI and machine learning tools to track trends in collections, predict potential delinquencies, and identify patterns in customer behaviour. These tools can also suggest proactive measures based on historical data.

11.10   Supporting Customers with Genuine Intent to Pay

1. Flexible Repayment Options

- **Tailored Payment Plans:** Offer payment plans that suit the customer's financial situation, including deferral options, EMI restructuring, or lower interest rates to make payments more manageable.

2. Financial Education

- **Guidance on Financial Health:** Educate customers about budgeting, saving, and managing debt, helping them avoid future delinquencies. Financial literacy campaigns can help customers improve their long-term financial stability.

3. Empathetic Communication

- **Understanding the Customer's Situation:** Acknowledge the challenges the customer faces, whether they are personal or financial, and offer real solutions that can bring relief.

4. **Continuous Engagement**

- **Ongoing Follow-Ups:** Keep the communication lines open by providing regular follow-ups and reminders. Consistent engagement helps the customer feel supported and motivated to clear their dues.

Early delinquency collections require a balanced approach of proactive management, empathy, and legal diligence. By tracking delinquencies accurately, implementing tailored communication strategies, training field agents effectively, and supporting customers with genuine intentions to repay, banks can ensure healthier portfolios, maintain customer trust, and improve overall recovery rates. With clear goals, well-managed processes, and focused efforts, the bank will be able to mitigate risk and reduce potential losses.

12

Hard Bucket Collections Strategy

Comprehensive Management of 90+ DPD Cases and NPA Mitigation

Hard bucket collections, referring to loans overdue by 90 days or more, represent a critical juncture in a bank's credit lifecycle. These loans are at high risk of becoming irrecoverable, directly impacting a bank's profitability, reputation, and compliance. To effectively manage these accounts, a holistic strategy is essential—balancing empathetic customer engagement, rigorous tracking mechanisms, legal actions, and well-defined supervisory roles.

Below is an elaborated point-by-point strategy for hard bucket collections.

12.1 Importance of Hard Bucket Collections

1. **Financial Impact on Banks**

   - **Capital Allocation Stress:** NPAs require provisioning as per regulatory guidelines, tying up funds that could be used for profitable lending. For instance, a 90+ DPD account categorized as "Substandard" may require 15% provisioning, increasing as it ages.

- **Erosion of Revenue:** Banks lose interest income on these accounts as they cease to be revenue-generating assets. Additionally, recovery efforts may involve litigation, repossession, or auction costs.

- **Operational Costs:** Managing hard buckets involves costs like field visits, legal proceedings, and asset repossession, which are higher than early-stage delinquencies.

2. **Regulatory Compliance**

- **Provisioning Norms:** Regulatory bodies like RBI mandate specific provisioning based on asset classification. Effective hard bucket collections can reduce NPAs, thereby lowering these provisions.

- **Reporting Standards:** Accurate reporting to regulatory authorities and credit bureaus is crucial. Delays in reporting or resolution could invite penalties or reputational damage.

3. **Portfolio Health and Bank Reputation**

- **Maintaining Portfolio Quality:** Prompt action on 90+ DPD accounts ensures better control of the loan book and prevents further deterioration of asset quality.

- **Reputation Management:** Handling accounts in this stage with fairness and efficiency reinforces the bank's reputation as customer-centric while demonstrating strong governance.

12.2 Tracking Mechanisms for Hard Bucket Cases

1. Centralized Data Management

- **Integrated Loan Management System (LMS):** Utilize systems to track customer interactions, payments, legal status, and resolution progress in real time.

- **Classification by Severity:** Segment NPAs into sub-categories: Substandard (90–12 months overdue), Doubtful (over 12 months overdue), and Loss assets. This helps prioritize recovery efforts.

2. Predictive Analytics

- **AI-Driven Insights:** Use predictive models to analyse customer behaviour, repayment capacity, and intent. This data-driven prioritization ensures field teams focus on accounts with the highest recovery potential.

- **Risk Scoring:** Assign risk scores to NPAs, guiding the escalation of accounts needing legal intervention or other measures.

3. Real-Time Monitoring

- **Geo-Tagged Tracking for Field Agents:** Deploy geo-tagging tools to monitor field agents' visits, ensuring on-ground effectiveness.

- **Real-Time Updates:** Field agents must update the system immediately after each visit, recording customer commitments, disputes, or situational details.

4. **Legal Action Tracker**

   - **Centralized Legal Repository:** Maintain a repository to monitor case progress for accounts under litigation, arbitration, or SARFAESI actions.

   - **Escalation Metrics:** Define timelines for escalating unresolved cases, ensuring no delays in recovery efforts.

12.3   Strategies for Hard Bucket Collections

1. **Customer Communication and Engagement**

   - **Tailored Communication:** Use data insights to address specific customer pain points. For example, address queries about penalties, resolve disputes, or provide tailored repayment plans.

   - **Empathy in Communication:** Treat genuine customers with respect to maintain relationships and avoid reputational harm. Use phrases like, "Let's find a way to resolve this together," rather than aggressive language.

2. **Field Collection Strategies**

   - **Dedicated Senior Executives:** Assign experienced agents for handling 90+ DPD accounts. Their expertise in negotiation and persuasion can lead to quicker resolutions.

   - **Structured Follow-Up Plan:** Plan frequent, structured follow-ups with set goals for each visit, ensuring no customer is left unchecked.

3. **Legal Tools and Actions**

   - **Issuing Legal Notices:**

     - **Section 138 (Negotiable Instruments Act):** For bounced cheques, initiate proceedings to hold defaulters accountable.

     - **Demand Notices:** Notify customers about overdue amounts with a defined compliance timeframe to signal seriousness.

   - **SARFAESI Actions:**

     - **Asset Possession and Sale:** Use SARFAESI Act provisions to repossess and auction secured assets without requiring court intervention.

     - **Compliance with Timelines:** Issue a 60-day demand notice, followed by possession and auction notices as per SARFAESI rules.

   - **Debt Recovery Tribunals (DRT):** For high-value accounts, file cases with DRT for specialized and quicker resolutions compared to traditional courts.

   - **Lok Adalat and Arbitration:** Explore these alternative dispute resolution mechanisms to settle smaller loans or contractual disputes.

4. **Skip Tracing**

   - **Advanced Tools:** Use technology-driven tools to locate absconding customers, integrating databases like telecom records, public registries, and social media analytics.

- **Third-Party Agencies:** Employ skip-tracing professionals for cases beyond internal tracking capabilities.

5. **Settlements and Restructuring**

- **One-Time Settlement (OTS):** Offer realistic settlements to avoid prolonged litigation costs while recovering a reasonable portion of the overdue amount.

- **EMI Restructuring:** For cooperative customers, restructure EMIs to align with their current financial capacity.

12.4   Handling Intentional Defaulters

1. **Identifying Wilful Defaulters**

- **Behavioural Analysis:** Look for patterns like shifting addresses without notice, transferring secured assets, or avoiding communication consistently.

- **Investigative Techniques:** Use financial forensics to trace misappropriation of funds or diversion of loans.

2. **Stronger Legal Actions**

- **Public Notices:** Publish defaulter details (within legal limits) in newspapers to deter further defaults and pressure recovery.

- **Attachment of Assets:** Initiate legal actions for asset attachment under applicable laws to recover dues.

12.5 Supervisory Role in Hard Bucket Management

1. Field Staff Monitoring

- **Regular Performance Reviews:** Conduct daily reviews of field executives' productivity using KPIs like visits completed, recovery amounts, and agreements secured.

- **Geo-Tracking Audits:** Supervisors must ensure field agents adhere to assigned schedules and are genuinely engaging with customers.

2. Training and Skill Enhancement

- **Legal Awareness Training:** Equip field agents with knowledge about legal recovery tools like SARFAESI, Section 138, and arbitration.

- **Negotiation Skills:** Teach advanced negotiation techniques to recover dues without escalating disputes unnecessarily.

3. Target Setting and Motivation

- **SMART Goals:** Set Specific, Measurable, Achievable, Relevant, and Time-bound (SMART) targets for field teams to encourage focused recovery efforts.

- **Incentive Programs:** Provide monetary incentives for field executives achieving high-resolution rates or significant recoveries.

12.6   Techniques to Track Productivity

1. **Key Performance Indicators (KPIs)**

   - **Resolution Rate:** Percentage of 90+ DPD cases resolved within a specified timeframe.

   - **Recovery Ratio:** Total amount recovered versus total overdue amount.

   - **Visit Completion Rate:** Percentage of scheduled visits completed as planned.

2. **Technology Integration**

   - **Mobile Apps:** Equip field staff with apps for real-time updates on case status, payment commitments, and geo-tagged visit logs.

   - **Analytics Dashboards:** Supervisors can use dashboards to monitor field productivity and identify underperforming agents.

12.7   Supporting Customers in Genuine Distress

1. **Financial Counselling**

   - **One-on-One Discussions:** Provide dedicated counselling sessions for customers facing financial hardships. Help them plan budgets and prioritize payments.

   - **Flexible Payment Options:** Offer short-term relief measures like partial payments or deferred EMIs for cooperative customers.

2. **Empathetic Approach**

   - **Understanding Root Causes:** Investigate reasons for default, whether due to medical emergencies, job loss, or business downturns, and provide tailored solutions.

   - **Preserving Customer Dignity:** Handle interactions tactfully to maintain customer trust and avoid reputational risks.

12.8   Benefits of Effective Hard Bucket Management

- **Reduction in GNPA Ratios:** A proactive approach ensures fewer accounts transition into higher-risk categories, stabilizing the bank's GNPA.

- **Improved Financial Stability:** Recovering overdue amounts restores the bank's liquidity and lending capacity.

- **Customer Retention:** Empathetic handling of genuine cases fosters long-term customer loyalty.

Managing hard bucket collections is a complex but essential process requiring a combination of human empathy, robust tracking mechanisms, and legal acumen. By adopting the strategies outlined above, banks and NBFCs can mitigate financial losses, comply with regulatory norms, and reinforce customer trust.

13

Repossession of Vehicle Strategy

Repossession of a vehicle, while an available tool for recovery in the lending ecosystem, is the last resort for any bank or NBFC. It impacts both the bank and the customer significantly. The goal should be to repossess not just the asset but also the customer's trust wherever feasible. However, repossession becomes necessary in cases of wilful defaults to safeguard the financial health of the institution.

Below is a detailed perspective from the bank's and the customer's point of view, along with an in-depth strategy for vehicle repossession.

13.1   Why Repossession Should Be the Last Resort?

From the Bank's Perspective:

1. Loss of Customer Relationship:

Repossessing a vehicle often terminates the relationship with the customer, impacting long-term cross-selling or up-selling opportunities.

The bank may lose goodwill in the market, especially if the customer feels unjustly treated.

2. Cost Implications:

Operational Costs: Deploying agents for repossession incurs costs for logistics, manpower, and potential legal expenses.

Storage and Maintenance: Banks incur costs in storing repossessed vehicles until auction or resale.

Auction Losses: Recovered vehicles often sell at a price below the outstanding loan amount, creating a financial gap.

3. Reputational Risk:

Aggressive repossession practices can tarnish the bank's reputation, leading to negative publicity and customer distrust.

4. Regulatory Compliance:

Mishandling repossession can lead to legal disputes and penalties, as financial institutions are required to follow due process strictly.

From the Customer's Perspective:

1. Loss of Livelihood:

Many borrowers rely on their vehicles for their income (e.g., truck drivers, delivery personnel). Losing the vehicle often leads to financial devastation.

2. Emotional Impact:

Repossession can lead to embarrassment and stress, especially in cases where financial troubles are beyond the customer's control (e.g., medical emergencies, job loss).

3. Credit Bureau Impact:

A repossession is reported to credit bureaus, significantly damaging the customer's credit score and limiting future access to credit.

4. Trust Deficit:

Customers may feel betrayed by the institution, especially if they were willing to pay but could not meet short-term obligations.

Principles of Repossession Strategy

- **Empathy First:** Understand the customer's situation before initiating any repossession action.

- **Clarity of Intent:** Repossession should be pursued only when there is clear evidence of intentional default or complete non-cooperation.

- **Compliance with Laws:** Follow all regulatory guidelines and ethical practices to ensure fair treatment.

- **Preserving Customer Trust:** Treat the process as a last measure while prioritizing customer retention and repayment solutions.

13.2   Repossession Strategy: Step-by-Step Approach

Pre-Repossession Stage: Preventive Measures

1. Early Engagement with Customers:

Identify delinquent customers early (60–90 DPD) and prioritize resolution through dialogue.

Use digital channels (voice bots, WhatsApp bots, SMS) to send reminders and offer repayment solutions.

2. Customized Repayment Plans:

Offer flexible payment options like EMI restructuring, moratoriums, or partial payment acceptance to ease the burden on genuine customers.

3. Understanding Customer Intent:

Behavioural Assessment: Analyse payment patterns, complaints, or disputes. Genuine customers may request time or provide proof of hardships.

Wilful Defaulters: Focus repossession efforts on customers who exhibit avoidance behaviour, provide false promises, or refuse to cooperate.

4. Customer Counselling:

Provide one-on-one sessions for distressed customers to explore options like refinancing or debt restructuring.

Emphasize the repercussions of repossession, such as credit score impact and loss of vehicle utility.

Decision to Repossess

1. Indicators for Repossession:

Multiple failed follow-ups with no response or resolution.

Verified intent of the customer to avoid payment (e.g., asset misuse or fraudulent practices).

Legal disputes that cannot be resolved amicably.

2. Approval Process:

Require multi-level approvals for repossession to ensure all alternatives have been explored.

Document all interactions, efforts, and reasons for repossession to ensure transparency.

Repossession Process

1. Legal and Ethical Compliance:

Follow guidelines under the SARFAESI Act or other applicable laws.

Ensure the repossession agency is certified and adheres to ethical practices.

2. Notification to the Customer:

Serve a clear and detailed notice to the customer, explaining the outstanding amount, steps to avoid repossession, and deadlines.

Provide a final opportunity for the customer to resolve the dues before initiating repossession.

2. Engaging Professional Agencies:

Use experienced and professional repossession agencies who understand the importance of customer interaction during asset recovery.

Ensure agents conduct themselves respectfully, avoiding coercion or conflict.

3. Transparent Execution:

Involve local authorities if needed to avoid disputes or escalations during repossession.

Record the entire process for accountability.

Post-Repossession Stage

1. Customer Communication:

Inform the customer of the repossession outcome, outstanding dues, and potential legal actions.

Offer an option for the customer to reclaim the vehicle by clearing dues within a specified timeframe.

2. Asset Management:

Conduct a thorough assessment of the repossessed vehicle for its condition and market value.

Maintain proper documentation and storage of the vehicle.

3. Disposal of Vehicle:

Auction Process: Conduct fair and transparent auctions to maximize recovery value.

Direct Sale: In cases where auctions are not feasible, consider direct sale to third parties while complying with regulatory norms.

Legal Tools for Repossession Strategy

In repossession strategies, leveraging legal tools ensures compliance with laws and builds a framework for ethical and effective recovery. Legal instruments provide banks and NBFCs with a structured approach to handle delinquent cases while mitigating risks of disputes. Here's a detailed breakdown of key legal tools for repossession:

SARFAESI Act (Securitisation and Reconstruction of Financial Assets and Enforcement of Security Interest Act, 2002)

- **Applicability:**

Pertains to secured loans where the vehicle or asset is pledged as collateral.

Enables lenders to recover dues by taking possession of the secured asset and auctioning it without requiring court intervention.

- **Key Provisions for Repossession:**

Demand Notice:

- A demand notice under Section 13(2) must be issued to the borrower, giving a 60-day period to regularize payments.

Possession of Asset:

- If the borrower fails to comply within the notice period, the lender can take symbolic or physical possession under Section 13(4).

Auction Process:

The repossessed asset is auctioned to recover dues.

Transparent valuation and auction procedures must be followed to ensure compliance and fairness.

- **Benefits:**

  - Expedites recovery by bypassing court delays.

  - Reduces operational costs associated with legal proceedings.

- **Best Practices:**

  - Ensure proper documentation, including loan agreements and demand notices, to prevent disputes.

  - Conduct repossession with sensitivity to avoid reputational risks.

Section 138 of the Negotiable Instruments Act (Cheque Bounce Cases)

- **Applicability:**

  - Covers cases where post-dated repayment cheques issued by borrowers are dishonoured due to insufficient funds or other reasons.

- **Key Provisions:**

  1. **Notice to Borrower:**

     - Issue a written demand notice to the borrower within 30 days of cheque dishonour.

     - The borrower is given 15 days to settle the dues.

  2. **Filing a Complaint:**

     - If the borrower fails to respond, initiate a criminal complaint in court under Section 138.

  3. **Penalties:**

     - Conviction can lead to fines, imprisonment, or both, motivating borrowers to resolve dues promptly.

- **Benefits:**

  - Acts as a deterrent for borrowers attempting to evade repayment.

  - Provides legal leverage to recover dues without repossession.

- **Best Practices:**

  - Maintain proper records of cheques and dishonour slips to strengthen the case.

  - opt for amicable settlements wherever possible before escalating to court.

13.2.1   Court-Ordered Repossession

- **Applicability:**

  - Used for unsecured loans, contested repossessions, or cases where borrowers challenge the repossession process.

- **Process:**

  1. **Filing a Case:**

     - Approach civil courts to obtain an order for repossession, ensuring legal backing for asset recovery.

  2. **Execution of Court Order:**

     - Engage authorized personnel to carry out repossession under judicial supervision.

  3. **Handling Disputes:**

     - Court orders minimize disputes by providing a legal basis for recovery actions.

- **Benefits:**

    o   Provides legitimacy in contentious cases, reducing the risk of legal retaliation.

    o   Protects the institution's reputation by ensuring due process.

- **Best Practices:**

    o   Use court-ordered repossession as a last resort after exhausting all pre-litigation options.

    o   Ensure compliance with timelines and judicial directives to avoid delays.

13.2.2   Lok Adalat and Arbitration

- **Applicability:**

    o   Effective for small-ticket loans and disputes where borrowers are willing to negotiate but require legal validation for resolutions.

- **Process:**

1. **Lok Adalat:**

    o   Forums for out-of-court settlements under Section 19 of the Legal Services Authorities Act, 1987.

    o   Helps resolve disputes quickly and amicably without legal fees or prolonged litigation.

2. **Arbitration:**

- ○ Resolve disputes through arbitration clauses in loan agreements.

- ○ Arbitration awards are legally enforceable, providing a swift resolution mechanism.

- **Benefits:**

- ○ Reduces the burden of litigation on courts and financial institutions.

- ○ Promotes goodwill by resolving disputes in a collaborative manner.

- **Best Practices:**

- ○ Train legal and recovery teams to identify cases suitable for Lok Adalat or arbitration.

- ○ Maintain a transparent process to build trust with borrowers.

13.2.3   Additional Legal Tools and Techniques

Repossession Authorization

- ○ Secure agreements with certified repossession agencies that adhere to legal norms.

- ○ Ensure agents are trained on compliance to minimize risks of illegal or unethical practices.

Public Notices

- Publish notices in newspapers before auctioning repossessed assets to meet legal requirements.

- Ensures transparency and allows borrowers an additional opportunity to settle dues.

Credit Bureau Reporting

- Use credit bureau reporting as a deterrent for defaults, as poor credit scores can affect borrowers' financial future.

- Ensure timely updates to credit bureaus to maintain compliance.

Legal tools for repossession are critical for structured and compliant asset recovery. Institutions must strike a balance between leveraging these tools effectively and maintaining a customer-centric approach to preserve trust and reputation. By adhering to legal frameworks, banks and NBFCs can achieve successful recovery outcomes while upholding ethical standards.

13.3 Supervisory Role in Repossession

1. **Guiding Field Teams:**

   - Supervisors must train field agents on ethical practices, customer handling, and compliance.

   - Regularly review agent performance and ensure repossession decisions align with bank policies.

2. **Monitoring Compliance:**

   - Ensure all repossession activities are well-documented and meet regulatory requirements.

   - Audit processes periodically to avoid reputational or legal risks.

3. **Post-Repossession Review:**

   - Analyse repossession outcomes to identify gaps in the pre-repossession stage, improving strategies for the future.

13.4 Supporting Genuine Customers Post-Repossession

- **Opportunities for Reinstatement:**

  - Offer repossessed vehicles back to genuine customers through tailored repayment plans or partial settlements.

- **Credit Counselling:**

  - Guide customers on rebuilding their creditworthiness post-repossession.

13.5 Metrics for Effective Repossession Management

1. **Resolution Rates:** Percentage of repossession cases resolved amicably or through partial payment agreements.

2. **Recovery Efficiency:** Amount recovered as a percentage of the outstanding dues.

3. **Customer Retention:** Percentage of customers re-engaged post-repossession through refinancing or other means.

4. **Compliance Score:** Adherence to legal and ethical guidelines in repossession activities.

Repossession is a delicate process that must be handled with empathy, fairness, and strategic rigor. By focusing on recovering both the asset and the customer relationship, banks and NBFCs can mitigate financial losses while maintaining their reputation as responsible lenders.

"Data is the new oil."

— Clive Humby

- **Attributed to:** Clive Humby, a British mathematician and data scientist, known for his work on Tesco's Clubcard.

- **Background:** This quote highlights the growing importance of data in driving insights and strategies. In collections, advanced analytics powered by data is now central to optimizing recovery processes.

14

Advanced Analytics for Enhanced Collections Efficiency

Advanced Analytics for Enhanced Collections Efficiency leverages sophisticated data models, machine learning algorithms, and predictive analytics to revolutionize collections strategies. By analysing vast amounts of customer data, including payment history, transaction patterns, demographic information, and external factors such as economic conditions, advanced analytics enables financial institutions to identify high-risk accounts and prioritize them for proactive engagement. Predictive models anticipate customer behaviour, allowing banks to forecast delinquency patterns and customize interventions accordingly. Additionally, real-time insights into customer behaviour and payment trends allow collections teams to tailor communication strategies, whether through phone, email, or digital channels, to maximize recovery rates. This data-driven approach not only enhances the efficiency of collections efforts but also improves customer satisfaction by offering personalized solutions, reducing manual intervention, and driving cost-effective decision-making.

14.1 Customer Segmentation Analytics

Customer segmentation is the foundation for prioritizing collection efforts. By categorizing customers based on their payment behaviour and risk, banks can allocate resources effectively.

Detailed Use case:

1. Prioritizing Efforts: Focus on High-Value or High-Risk Accounts First

Prioritizing efforts based on account value and risk ensures that resources are allocated effectively to maximize recovery and reduce delinquency rates.

Detailed Explanation:

- **High-Value Accounts:**

  - These are accounts with large loan amounts or high financial exposure.

  - Delinquency in such accounts poses a significant risk to the financial stability of the portfolio.

  - Analytics helps identify these accounts early, enabling focused efforts to recover or regularize them.

- **High-Risk Accounts:**

  - Customers showing signs of potential default (e.g., inconsistent payment patterns or poor credit scores).

  - Accounts with prior delinquencies or customers operating in volatile industries.

  - Analytics enables predictive modelling to flag accounts likely to escalate into higher DPD buckets, allowing proactive intervention.

Key Metrics Used for Prioritization:

1. Outstanding Loan Amount: High-value loans take precedence.

2. Bureau Scores: Low scores indicate higher risk.

3. Delinquency History: Frequent past delays signal a risk of default.

4. Income to EMI Ratio: High ratios highlight repayment challenges.

5. Industry Risk: Customers in struggling sectors (e.g., tourism during a pandemic).

6. Loan Tenure: Short-term loans may require faster intervention due to limited recovery windows.

Execution Approach:

- Create a tiered priority system (e.g., Tier 1 for high-value, Tier 2 for high-risk).

- Assign specialized agents to handle top-priority accounts.

- Develop detailed action plans for each priority category, including customized communication and follow-up schedules.

2. Tailoring Communication: Personalized Approaches Based on Customer Segments

Personalized communication increases the likelihood of engaging with customers and encouraging repayment by addressing their unique needs and challenges.

Detailed Explanation:

- **Segment-Based Messaging:**

  - Customers with different risk profiles require different tones and channels of communication.

  - For low-risk, temporary delinquencies: Use empathetic messaging to remind customers of missed payments.

  - For high-risk or chronic defaulters: Use firm but respectful reminders emphasizing consequences.

- **Language and Tone Customization:**
    - Use local languages or dialects for better customer understanding.
    - Adjust tone based on customer history (e.g., reassuring for first-time defaulters, assertive for repeat defaulters).

- **Channel Preferences:**
    - Digital channels (SMS, email, WhatsApp) for tech-savvy customers.
    - Call center or field visits for customers less comfortable with technology.

Execution Approach:

1. Segment customers into groups (e.g., high-risk, low-risk, chronic, first-time defaulters).

2. Use data to craft templates tailored to each group.

3. Leverage automated communication tools (chatbots, voice bots) for large-scale personalized outreach.

4. Continuously refine messaging based on response rates and feedback.

Example Scenarios:

- A salaried customer missing one EMI due to a temporary liquidity crunch receives a polite reminder offering partial payment options.

- A high-risk customer with repeated defaults receives firm communication outlining repossession or legal implications.

3. Defining Allocation: Assigning Customers to Call Centres, Field Agents, or Digital Channels

Effective allocation ensures that resources (human and technological) are deployed where they can make the most impact, balancing efficiency and cost.

Detailed Explanation:

- **Call Centres for Early Delinquency:**
  - Handle first-time or low-risk delinquencies to regularize payments through reminders.
  - Utilize automated diallers and voice bots for high-volume, low-cost communication.

- **Field Agents for High-Risk Accounts:**
  - Deploy for accounts requiring physical intervention, such as high-value loans or chronic defaulters.
  - Assign agents based on geographic proximity to minimize travel costs and time.

- **Digital Channels for Tech-Savvy Customers:**
  - Use SMS, email, or WhatsApp for reminders and payment links.
  - Enable instant payment options through integrated apps or UPI systems.

Key Metrics for Allocation Decisions:

1. Delinquency Stage: 0-30 DPD (call centres), 30+ DPD (field agents).
2. Account Value: High-value accounts to field agents or specialized teams.

3. Customer Responsiveness: Non-responsive customers escalated to field agents.

4. Regional Distribution: Cluster accounts geographically for efficient field operations.

5. Communication Preference: Tech-savvy customers allocated to digital channels.

Execution Approach:

1. Analyse the portfolio to segment customers based on risk, value, and behaviour.

2. Allocate resources dynamically based on daily/weekly portfolio changes.

3. Use CRM tools to assign cases and monitor progress in real time.

4. Continuously evaluate allocation efficiency and reassign resources as needed.

Example Scenarios:

- A low-value, low-risk account at 15 DPD is handled by a call center agent using automated reminders.

- A high-value customer at 60 DPD receives a field visit to understand the repayment challenges and negotiate terms.

- A tech-savvy customer at 25 DPD is sent an automated WhatsApp message with an instant payment link.

By leveraging these use cases, banks and NBFCs can optimize collections efforts, reduce costs, and improve customer relationships while maintaining a healthy portfolio.

Key Variables for Risk Categorization

1. **Repayment History:** On-time payments, delays, or defaults.

2. **Loan Tenure:** Loan age vs. time left for maturity.

3. **Loan Amount:** High-value loans require closer monitoring.

4. **Customer Income:** Verified income and debt-to-income ratio.

5. **Employment Type:** Salaried, self-employed, or unemployed.

6. **Bureau Score:** Historical credit behaviour and defaults.

7. **Account Activity:** Deposit trends, withdrawals, and anomalies.

8. **Geo-Location:** High-risk regions vs. stable economic zones.

9. **Communication History:** Responsiveness to reminders or calls.

10. **Demographics:** Age, gender, and family size (to gauge dependencies).

14.2 Strategy-Based Contact Review

A structured review ensures that collection strategies are applied consistently and effectively across all cases.

Use Cases

1. Supervisory Insights: Helps Supervisors Intervene Where Necessary

Supervisors play a crucial role in maintaining efficiency and addressing roadblocks in collections. Analytics-driven insights enable supervisors to intervene precisely where needed to enhance resolution rates and mitigate escalations.

Detailed Points:

- **Proactive Monitoring:**

    o   Supervisors gain real-time visibility into key metrics such as contact rates, resolution rates, and pending cases.

    o   Alerts for deviations from standard performance benchmarks allow timely interventions.

- **Focused Escalation Management:**

    o   High-risk accounts are flagged for supervisory attention to assess the need for escalations or alternative strategies (e.g., restructuring or repossession).

    o   Supervisors can mediate between customers and field agents for amicable resolutions.

- **Feedback Mechanism:**

    o   Supervisors can review field visit notes or call recordings to evaluate communication quality.

    o   Immediate feedback can be provided to agents for improvement.

- **Customized Guidance:**

  - Supervisors can identify agents struggling with specific customer segments or regions and provide tailored coaching.

- **Improved Resource Allocation:**

  - Insights help supervisors reallocate resources dynamically based on workload and case criticality.

2. Uniform Review: Avoids Bias and Ensures Uniformity in Assessments

Uniform review processes ensure all accounts are assessed objectively, minimizing bias and driving consistency across the collections team.

Detailed Points:

- **Standardized Criteria:**

  - Use predefined metrics (e.g., payment history, bounce patterns, risk scores) to uniformly evaluate customer accounts.

  - Rule-based triggers initiate reviews automatically, avoiding subjectivity.

- **Fair Escalation and Allocation:**

  - Cases are flagged for escalation based on risk level, regardless of customer profile or location, ensuring no account is overlooked.

  - Uniformity in case prioritization leads to better resource utilization.

- **Improved Decision-Making:**

  - Supervisors rely on data-driven insights rather than personal judgment, which increases transparency and trust within the team.

- **Enhanced Team Performance:**

  - Uniform review processes highlight systemic issues, such as common customer complaints or recurring delays, which can be addressed through policy changes.

3. Field Support: Identifies Field Agents Needing Training or Resources

Efficient collections depend on the performance of field agents, who are often the first point of contact with customers. Identifying agents needing support ensures the team functions optimally.

Detailed Points:

- **Performance Analytics:**

  - Analyse key metrics for field agents such as daily visit targets, payment pickup success rates, and customer contact efficiency.

  - Flagging underperforming agents helps supervisors pinpoint issues early.

- **Skill Gap Identification:**

  - Track trends in missed collections or customer complaints linked to specific agents.

   o   Supervisors can identify agents needing training in negotiation, communication, or technical tools.

- **Resource Allocation:**

   o   Ensure agents have the tools they need, such as updated customer data, mobility solutions, or transportation support.

   o   Address logistical challenges like inadequate regional coverage or long travel distances.

- **Motivation and Retention:**

   o   Regular reviews can identify high-performing agents, enabling supervisors to reward and motivate them.

   o   Personalized guidance and support for low performers foster morale and reduce attrition.

Execution Steps:

1. Develop dashboards to track agent-level metrics such as visit success rate and customer feedback.

2. Conduct monthly review meetings to assess individual performance and training needs.

3. Implement reward programs for high-performing agents to set benchmarks for the team.

4. Organize targeted training programs based on identified skill gaps.

By focusing on these areas, supervisors can drive efficiency, ensure fairness, and support field agents in achieving better collection outcomes.

Key Variables for Strategy-Based Contact Review

1. **Resolution Rates:** Success rates of individual agents or teams.

2. **PTP (Promise to Pay) Fulfilment:** Customers honouring commitments.

3. **Follow-Up Timeliness:** Adherence to timelines for calls and visits.

4. **Customer Feedback:** Insights from customer surveys or interactions.

5. **Agent Productivity:** Accounts handled vs. resolved.

6. **Behavioural Metrics:** Agent attitude and adherence to processes.

7. **Escalation Cases:** Number of cases flagged for higher-level attention.

8. **Field Visit Outcomes:** Success rates from physical customer interactions.

Strategy-Based Escalations

Exception handling is critical in collections. Automated escalation rules ensure timely intervention by higher authorities.

Use Cases for Identifying, Managing, and Supervising Collection Cases:

1. Identifying Issues: Highlighting Cases Stuck in the Pipeline

The primary goal of this use case is to identify collection cases that are stagnating or stuck in the pipeline, which could potentially lead to greater delinquency and negative impact on the portfolio. This can be achieved through advanced analytics tools, which track the status and progress of each case in real-time. By analysing historical data, transaction timelines, and customer responses, the system can automatically flag cases that have not progressed as expected. This could include cases where customers have not responded to collection attempts, cases where payments are overdue without resolution, or instances where the contact information is outdated or incorrect. Identifying these issues early allows the collections team to focus on them before they worsen, ensuring that no case remains dormant or overlooked for extended periods.

Key Features:

- Real-time tracking and monitoring of customer cases.

- Flags for delays in contact attempts, payments, or legal actions.

- Identification of gaps in customer communication or resolution actions.

- Risk-based prioritization of unresolved cases based on customer history.

2. Timely Action: Avoiding Delays in High-Priority Cases

For high-priority cases, it is crucial to take prompt action to avoid further delinquency or escalation. This use case revolves around the timely intervention of the collections team, ensuring that cases with significant risk of default or financial loss are addressed immediately. By implementing rule-based automation or AI-driven alerts, the system can identify accounts that are approaching critical delinquency thresholds, such as 90+ DPD, and generate a prioritized task list for the collections team. The system can also automate some aspects of customer engagement, such as reminders and payment offer, but it is essential for human agents to step in at the right time to offer personalized assistance, payment restructuring, or legal action if necessary. This ensures that high-priority cases don't slip through the cracks and are handled in a timely manner to maximize recovery and prevent them from moving further into default.

Key Features:

- Real-time alerts for accounts approaching critical stages (e.g., 60 or 90 DPD).

- Prioritized task list for collections teams.

- Automation of initial outreach for quicker action.

- Seamless integration of automated actions with human follow-ups for personalized engagement.

3. Supervisor Oversight: Ensures Accountability at Every Level

Effective collections management requires constant oversight to ensure that all cases are being handled appropriately and efficiently. Supervisor oversight ensures accountability at every level of the collections process. By monitoring the performance of individual agents and the resolution progress of cases, supervisors can identify areas where agents may need additional training, resources, or guidance. Supervisors can also ensure that policies and procedures are being followed, avoiding potential compliance risks or inconsistent approaches. Supervisory dashboards and reporting tools can provide real-time insights into key performance metrics, such as the number of calls made, collection rates, outstanding balances, and escalated cases. With this oversight, supervisors can provide corrective actions where necessary, ensuring that all accounts are being managed according to best practices and driving consistent results across the team.

Key Features:

- Real-time visibility into agent performance and case progression.

- Performance metrics tracking, including calls made, cases resolved, and targets met.

- Automated alerts to flag underperforming agents or unresolved cases.

- Centralized dashboards to track cases, actions, and supervisor involvement.

Summary of Use Case Impact:

By leveraging these use cases, collection teams can drive more effective and efficient recovery efforts. **Identifying issues** in the pipeline early leads to proactive intervention, while **timely action** ensures that high-priority cases are resolved quickly, preventing further loss. Finally, **supervisor oversight** not only enhances agent performance but also ensures compliance and accountability in every stage of the collections process, optimizing results and mitigating risks for the organization. This integrated approach allows banks and financial institutions to enhance recovery, reduce delinquencies, and maintain a more manageable risk profile.

Key Variables for Strategy-Based Escalations

1. **Delinquency Aging:** Cases beyond a certain threshold (e.g., 30+ DPD).

2. **Non-Responsive Customers:** Accounts with no customer contact.

3. **PTP Breaches:** Promises made but not fulfilled.

4. **High-Value Loans:** Accounts with significant financial exposure.

5. **Field Agent Challenges:** Cases flagged as difficult by agents.

6. **Customer Complaints:** Issues raised that need resolution.

7. **Legal Risks:** Customers threatening legal action against the bank.

14.4   Repossession Strategy

Analytics-driven repossession ensures minimal disruption while maximizing recoveries.

Use Cases for Repossession Strategy in Collections:

1. Pre-Repossession Analysis: Avoiding Unnecessary Repossessions

Before proceeding with repossession, it's vital to conduct a **pre-repossession analysis** to evaluate whether repossession is truly necessary or if alternative resolution methods can be employed. This use case focuses on assessing the viability of different recovery actions to avoid the financial and reputational costs associated with repossession. The analysis involves reviewing numerous factors such as the customer's payment history, reasons for default, current financial status, willingness to repay, and the potential to work out an arrangement like loan restructuring or payment plans.

Using analytics tools and customer data, the bank can predict which customers are more likely to cooperate if offered flexible repayment options. It's essential to prioritize customers who exhibit clear intentions to repay but may be facing temporary financial challenges, as these customers can be helped through guidance and alternative solutions without resorting to repossession.

Key Features:

- **Customer Payment History**: Review of past payments missed EMIs, and any pattern indicating financial hardship or temporary setbacks.

- **Financial Status Analysis**: Evaluating whether the customer's financial situation is likely to improve, which may allow them to repay in the future.

- **Intent to Repay**: Assessing the likelihood of the customer's willingness to settle their dues through alternative methods.

- **Alternative Recovery Options**: Identifying whether restructuring, renegotiation, or other non-repossession solutions are viable.

- **Cost-Benefit Analysis**: Calculating the costs associated with repossession vs. other alternatives (e.g., restructuring agreements, payment extensions).

2. Risk-Based Allocation: Identifying Accounts Where Repossession is Inevitable

Once the analysis of all available recovery alternatives is performed, the next step is to **identify high-risk accounts** where repossession may be inevitable. This use case focuses on leveraging data and analytics to assess risk and make informed decisions about which accounts to target for repossession. Factors such as customer's current default status (e.g., 90+ DPD), behaviour patterns, asset value, and legal considerations should all play a role in the decision-making process.

By applying predictive analytics, the system can assess the likelihood of full recovery through traditional collections methods. High-risk accounts, especially those with extended default periods or where the customer's financial distress is irreversible, should be flagged for repossession. This ensures that only accounts with minimal chance of recovery are considered for repossession, minimizing unnecessary actions.

Key Features:

- **Customer Risk Profiling**: Analysing customer behaviour, payment patterns, and historical defaults to predict future repayment likelihood.

- **Advanced Predictive Models**: Using AI and machine learning to identify customers likely to default further, allowing for more proactive and efficient decision-making.

- **Asset Value Assessment**: Evaluating the value of the asset in question to determine whether repossession is a cost-effective solution.

- **Legal Readiness**: Identifying accounts where the legal route is necessary for recovery, especially in cases of wilful default or disputed claims.

- **Optimization of Recovery Strategy**: Identifying accounts that will benefit from repossession over other collection strategies, ensuring a targeted approach.

3. Resource Optimization: Prioritizing Repossession of High-Value Assets

Repossession should focus on **high-value assets** to maximize recovery and minimize costs. This use case aims to optimize the resource allocation for repossession by prioritizing valuable assets that are worth recovering. By using advanced analytics to assess the asset's market value, condition, and potential resale value, the system can help the bank decide whether repossession will be financially worthwhile.

In many cases, the repossession process requires significant resources, including field agents, transportation, legal intervention, and storage costs. Therefore, prioritizing high-value assets—whether due to the value of the vehicle itself, the likelihood of quick resale, or its strategic importance to the bank's portfolio—ensures that the bank maximizes its return on investment (ROI). Low-value assets or those with a substantial risk of depreciation should be deprioritized or avoided in repossession.

Key Features:

- **Asset Value Determination**: Assessing the asset's market value and depreciation rate to ensure that the repossession is worth pursuing.

- **Depreciation Rate Modelling**: Predicting how much the asset will lose in value over time, allowing for timely repossession of high-value items.

- **Logistical Optimization**: Streamlining the repossession process to reduce costs associated with asset retrieval, storage, and transportation.

- **Recovery ROI Analysis**: Calculating the expected recovery vs. repossession costs to prioritize assets with the best ROI.

- **Regional Optimization**: Leveraging geographic and regional data to streamline repossession in areas where high-value assets are concentrated.

- **Legal Feasibility**: Identifying repossession opportunities where legal interventions can be applied effectively, ensuring that valuable assets can be recovered without unnecessary delays.

Summary of Use Case Impact:

By integrating these use cases into the repossession strategy, financial institutions can make more data-driven, cost-effective decisions when recovering assets. **Pre-repossession analysis** ensures that repossession is only pursued when necessary, preserving customer relationships where possible. **Risk-based allocation** optimizes the identification of accounts that require repossession, reducing inefficiencies and unnecessary actions. Finally, **resource optimization** ensures that the most valuable assets are prioritized for repossession, minimizing costs and maximizing recovery rates.

This strategy allows for smarter, more focused decision-making, helping banks and financial institutions to strike a balance between maintaining customer relationships and ensuring the efficient recovery of assets.

Key Variables for Repossession Strategy

1. **Asset Value:** Current market value vs. outstanding dues.

2. **Customer Intent:** Payment history and engagement levels.

3. **Economic Viability:** Cost of repossession vs. expected recovery.

4. **Legal Complications:** Risk of disputes or litigation.

5. **Field Feasibility:** Accessibility and risk in repossession operations.

6. **Asset Usage:** Commercial vs. personal use (commercial assets often have higher recovery potential).

7. **Post-Repossession Plan:** Likelihood of resale or redeployment of the asset.

Legal Strategy

Legal action is a critical component for addressing chronic defaulters. Analytics ensures that legal resources are deployed strategically.

Use Cases for Legal Strategy in Collections

1. Prioritizing Cases: Focus on Accounts with High Financial Exposure

In the context of collections, prioritizing accounts with high financial exposure ensures that limited legal resources are directed towards cases that present the greatest potential risk to the financial institution. Financial exposure refers to the total amount owed, including principal, interest, late fees, and other associated costs. When a customer's outstanding debt is substantial, the likelihood of recovery through legal means is higher, and the potential impact on the financial health of the institution is greater.

By using advanced analytics to assess financial exposure, the bank can identify accounts that represent the highest risk, allowing the legal team to prioritize them for immediate action.

This ensures that the legal resources are utilized effectively and that the most pressing cases are addressed first. For example, high-value accounts that are close to becoming non-performing assets (NPA) should be given more attention than smaller accounts that can potentially be resolved through less costly methods, such as negotiation or restructuring.

Key Features:

- **Outstanding Debt Assessment**: Quantifying the total financial exposure by calculating the principal, interest, penalties, and any other amounts due.

- **Risk-Based Prioritization**: Using predictive analytics to identify accounts at high risk of becoming NPAs and prioritize them based on the likelihood of default and exposure.

- **Portfolio Segmentation**: Categorizing accounts by risk, focusing on those that have high debt levels and are at risk of major financial losses.

- **Debt Collection and Legal Alignment**: Ensuring legal resources are allocated to the most critical accounts to optimize the chances of recovery.

- **Time Sensitivity**: Accounts with high exposure that are nearing the NPA threshold should be flagged for prompt legal action to avoid further deterioration.

2. Streamlining Processes: Automating Documentation for Legal Proceedings

The legal process can often be complex and time-consuming, with extensive documentation requirements for each case.

To expedite the legal proceedings and ensure accuracy, **automating documentation** plays a vital role in streamlining these processes. Automated systems can generate the required legal notices, contracts, claims, and court-related documents based on pre-defined templates and inputs.

By reducing the manual effort involved in preparing legal documents, automation not only saves time but also minimizes human errors that could compromise the effectiveness of the legal strategy. It can help in generating consistent and legally compliant documents, ensuring that they are submitted in a timely and accurate manner. Furthermore, automation can help track deadlines, reminders, and document statuses, ensuring that nothing is overlooked during the legal process.

Key Features:

- **Automated Document Generation**: Using automation tools to generate legal notices, recovery letters, default notifications, and other legal documents.

- **Data Integration**: Integrating customer data and contract details directly into legal templates to create personalized documents without manual input.

- **Compliance Check**: Automating the compliance verification process to ensure that all documents adhere to legal requirements and bank policies.

- **Document Workflow Automation**: Streamlining the approval and submission processes for legal documents, ensuring faster turnaround times.

- **Automated Deadlines & Reminders**: Setting up automated alerts for upcoming legal proceedings, deadlines for filing, and hearing dates, preventing missed opportunities.

3. Monitoring Legal Outcomes: Tracking the Effectiveness of Legal Interventions

Monitoring the effectiveness of legal actions is critical to ensuring that the bank's legal strategy delivers the desired outcomes. This involves tracking the success rates of various legal interventions, analysing their impact on debt recovery, and assessing their overall return on investment. Legal outcomes should not only be limited to successful repossessions or judgments but should also consider factors like the speed of resolution, the overall cost of legal proceedings, and customer response to legal actions.

By collecting and analysing data on the outcomes of legal interventions, the bank can refine its legal strategies over time. For example, if certain legal measures consistently result in quicker resolutions or better recovery rates, these approaches can be scaled and prioritized. On the other hand, ineffective strategies can be reevaluated or abandoned to improve the legal process. This ensures continuous optimization of the legal team's efforts and alignment with overall business objectives.

Key Features:

- **Legal Performance Metrics**: Tracking key performance indicators (KPIs) such as recovery amounts, case resolutions, and legal costs to evaluate the success of legal strategies.

- **Case Resolution Time**: Measuring the time taken from initiating legal action to achieving resolution (whether through repayment, settlement, or repossession).

- **Outcome Tracking**: Analysing the success rate of various legal tools such as arbitration, Lok Adalat, court orders, and repossession to determine their effectiveness.

- **Cost-Benefit Analysis**: Evaluating the cost of legal action versus the amount recovered, ensuring that the bank's resources are used efficiently.

- **Legal Channel Efficiency**: Assessing the performance of different legal channels (e.g., arbitration, Lok Adalat, court processes) to determine which offers the best recovery rates and cost-effectiveness.

- **Customer Response Data**: Monitoring how customers respond to legal actions (e.g., settlement, payment, engagement) to refine customer-specific legal strategies.

Summary of Use Case Impact:

By integrating these use cases into the **Legal Strategy**, the financial institution ensures that its legal resources are deployed in the most effective way possible.

- **Prioritizing cases** based on financial exposure allows the bank to focus on high-value and high-risk accounts, minimizing potential losses.

- **Streamlining processes** through automation ensures that legal documentation is accurate, consistent, and submitted promptly, reducing delays and human error.

- **Monitoring legal outcomes** provides the bank with data to continuously improve its legal strategy, making sure that the most effective legal tools and processes are being used.

These strategies help reduce the time and costs associated with legal proceedings, improve recovery rates, and ensure that the bank is adhering to regulatory and compliance standards. With a data-driven approach, the bank can make informed decisions and act proactively to resolve overdue accounts while maintaining customer relationships where possible.

Key Variables for Legal Strategy

1. **Loan Value:** High-value loans requiring legal intervention.

2. **Default History:** Repeated breaches of repayment commitments.

3. **Customer Intent:** Evidence of fraud or wilful default.

4. **Litigation Costs:** Expected costs vs. potential recovery.

5. **Legal Timelines:** Expected duration of proceedings.

6. **Asset Availability:** Ensuring repossessed assets are legally clear.

7. **Customer Communication:** Attempts to resolve amicably before legal action.

14.6   Predictive Analytics

Predictive analytics is a game-changer in preventing delinquency escalation.

Use Cases for Predictive Analytics in Collections

1. Default Likelihood: Identifying Customers Likely to Roll Forward into Higher DPD Buckets

Predicting which customers are at substantial risk of rolling forward into higher Days Past Due (DPD) buckets is crucial for efficient collections management. Early identification of such customers allows for proactive intervention, minimizing the impact on portfolio quality and preventing accounts from progressing to more serious stages of delinquency, such as 60+ DPD or 90+ DPD. By leveraging **predictive analytics**, the bank can use various data points to forecast the likelihood of a customer's account becoming severely delinquent.

Key Data Variables:

- **Payment History**: Previous payment patterns, such as late payments, partial payments, or missed payments, help identify customers with a tendency to delay payments.

- **Current DPD**: Customers with a 30 DPD or higher are more likely to roll forward into the next bucket if not managed properly.

- **Income Stability**: A customer's income history and job stability can be strong indicators of future repayment behaviour. A customer facing a potential job loss or income drop may be more likely to default.

- **Credit Utilization**: High utilization of available credit can indicate financial distress, increasing the likelihood of payment delays.

- **Recent Credit Inquiries**: Multiple recent inquiries for credit can signal financial distress and are often a precursor to payment delinquencies.

- **Customer Engagement**: Customers who are less engaged or responsive to communication efforts are more likely to default.

- **External Data**: Public records, such as bankruptcies, court judgments, or defaults in other institutions, can signal the risk of future delinquencies.

- **Account Type**: The type of loan (e.g., auto loan, personal loan, home loan) and its terms, such as interest rate and repayment schedule, affect the likelihood of default.

Use Case Application:

- **Early Intervention**: By using predictive models to assess default likelihood, collections teams can prioritize high-risk accounts for early outreach. For example, if a model identifies a customer in the 30-45 DPD bucket with a high probability of rolling forward to 60+ DPD, proactive communication (via call, SMS, email) and repayment options can be offered to mitigate the risk.

- **Customer Segmentation**: Based on likelihood scores, customers can be segmented into different risk groups, allowing for tailored collection strategies for each segment. For instance, high-risk customers may be flagged for immediate intervention, while low-risk customers may receive a more lenient approach.

Benefits:

- **Proactive Collections**: Reduces the chances of accounts slipping into higher DPD buckets by targeting high-risk customers before they fall further behind.

- **Reduced GNPA**: By preventing accounts from rolling into higher DPD buckets, the bank can improve its overall Non-Performing Asset (GNPA) ratio.

- **Optimized Resource Allocation**: Collections teams can focus their efforts on the most promising cases and allocate resources where they are most needed.

2. Payment Forecasting: Predicting Payment Timelines for Delinquent Accounts

Payment forecasting refers to predicting when a delinquent customer will likely make their next payment. This predictive approach is crucial for managing cash flow, setting realistic recovery expectations, and optimizing the collections process. By leveraging historical data, machine learning models, and customer behaviour insights, the bank can predict payment timelines for delinquent accounts with a high degree of accuracy.

Key Data Variables:

- **Payment History**: Analysing past payment trends to understand how long it typically takes for a customer to repay after defaulting.

- **Payment Frequency**: How often the customer has historically paid—whether they tend to make payments on the due date, early, or late—can be indicative of future payment behaviour.

- **Customer Communication**: Responses to past collection communications (calls, emails, SMS) can give clues about the likelihood of future payments. For example, if a customer often responds to reminders, they may be more likely to make timely payments in the future.

- **Income or Employment Status**: Changes in income or employment can be a major factor in predicting when a customer will be able to make a payment. For example, if a customer is recently employed after a period of unemployment, payment may be more likely within the next few months.

- **Account Aging**: The length of time the account has been delinquent can affect payment timing. For example, a customer who has been delinquent for 30 days may make a payment sooner than someone in the 90+ DPD bucket.

- **Customer Engagement**: Positive engagement, such as setting up payment plans or contacting customer service, can indicate the likelihood of future payments.

- **External Factors**: Economic indicators, such as inflation, unemployment rates, or changes in regulations, may also influence payment behaviour.

Use Case Application:

- **Cash Flow Management**: By accurately forecasting when payments will be received, the bank can plan for cash flow more effectively. For example, if payment forecasting indicates that a high percentage of delinquent customers will make payments in the next month, the bank can adjust its cash flow predictions accordingly.

- **Collections Strategy Adjustment**: Based on the forecasted payment dates, collections strategies can be adjusted. For instance, if a payment is expected soon, the focus may shift from aggressive recovery efforts to nurturing customer relationships, ensuring they remain compliant with their repayment schedule.

- **Payment Plan Optimization**: Payment forecasting can also help design more flexible payment plans based on the expected timing of a customer's repayment. For instance, a customer predicted to make a partial payment next month may be offered a structured plan to repay the remaining balance in instalments.

Benefits:

- **Improved Cash Flow Projections**: Enables more accurate cash flow management by predicting when payments will come in.

- **Increased Recovery Rates**: By identifying when payments are most likely to occur, the collections team can optimize their outreach and improve recovery rates.

- **Reduced Customer Frustration**: By predicting customer behaviour, the bank can avoid unnecessarily aggressive collections tactics on accounts that are likely to pay soon, leading to a better customer experience.

- **Optimized Resource Allocation**: Instead of wasting resources on high-cost recovery measures for accounts that will make a payment soon, efforts can be directed toward accounts with a longer repayment horizon.

Benefits of Combining Both Use Cases:

The combination of **default likelihood** and **payment forecasting** provides a comprehensive, data-driven approach to collections. Not only can the bank predict which accounts are at risk of deteriorating further, but it can also estimate when those accounts are likely to start repaying. This allows for a more targeted, proactive collections strategy that aligns with the customer's financial behaviour and minimizes operational costs.

In summary, **predictive analytics** can significantly improve the collections process by providing deeper insights into customer behaviour, enabling timely interventions, and helping institutions optimize recovery efforts.

Key Variables

1. **Repayment Trends:** Historical payment behaviour.

2. **Demographics:** Correlation between customer demographics and default.

3. **External Factors:** Economic indicators and industry trends.

4. **Communication Effectiveness:** Response patterns to reminders and calls.

14.7   Geo-Analytics for Field Efficiency

Field operations are critical in collections. Geo-analytics ensures optimal resource allocation.

Detailed Use Cases for Analytics in Collections

1. Route Optimization: Reducing Travel Time and Costs for Agents

Route optimization uses analytics and technology to plan the most efficient travel routes for field collection agents, ensuring that they can visit the maximum number of customers in the shortest time possible. This reduces operational costs, enhances productivity, and improves the overall efficiency of the collections process.

Key Features of Route Optimization:

- **Real-Time Data Integration**: Incorporates live traffic updates, weather conditions, and road closures to suggest the best routes dynamically.

- **Clustered Customer Visits**: Groups customer visits geographically to minimize travel time and fuel costs.

- **Priority-Based Routing**: Assigns higher priority to customers based on their risk scores or likelihood of resolution, ensuring the most critical accounts are visited first.

- **Dynamic Re-Routing**: Adjusts routes in real-time based on cancellations, no-shows, or updated priorities.

- **Distance and Time Tracking**: Tracks distances covered by agents and time spent on each visit to monitor productivity.

Benefits:

- **Reduced Operational Costs**: Minimizes fuel consumption and travel expenses, leading to significant cost savings.

- **Enhanced Productivity**: Allows agents to visit more customers in a day, improving their efficiency and increasing the likelihood of successful collections.

- **Timely Customer Interaction**: Enables agents to meet customers at optimal times, increasing the chances of payment recovery.

- **Reduced Carbon Footprint**: Optimized routes reduce unnecessary travel, contributing to a greener operational approach.

Example Scenario: An analytics-driven system clusters overdue accounts in a specific city and plans the day's visits for each agent, ensuring minimal backtracking. For instance, instead of visiting scattered customers, the system suggests visiting all overdue customers in a particular locality before moving to the next zone. This not only saves travel time but also increases the number of daily interactions.

2. Regional Analysis: Identifying High-Risk Zones

Regional analysis uses analytics to identify areas or zones with higher delinquency rates, allowing the collections team to allocate resources more effectively and tailor strategies to those regions. This ensures targeted interventions where they are most needed, improving recovery rates and optimizing the deployment of resources.

Key Features of Regional Analysis:

- **Delinquency Mapping**: Creates heat maps to visually represent zones with high concentrations of overdue accounts.

- **Behavioural Insights**: Analyses payment behaviours and risk factors specific to each region, such as local economic conditions, unemployment rates, or business shutdowns.

- **Zone Segmentation**: Categorizes regions into high-risk, medium-risk, and low-risk zones based on historical and real-time data.

- **Localized Strategies**: Adapts collection methods based on regional insights. For example, regions with higher intentional defaulters might require stricter follow-ups and legal interventions, while areas with cooperative customers may benefit from softer approaches.

- **Agent Deployment**: Prioritizes deploying field agents to high-risk zones where the probability of recovery is higher.

Benefits:

- **Targeted Resource Allocation**: Directs efforts to areas with the highest impact potential, avoiding unnecessary expenditure in low-risk zones.

- **Improved Recovery Rates**: Focused strategies in high-risk areas increase the chances of recovering overdue payments.

- **Tailored Communication**: Enables the design of region-specific communication strategies, such as language preferences or cultural considerations.

- **Trend Monitoring**: Tracks how delinquency rates in a region change over time, allowing for proactive measures in emerging high-risk zones.

Example Scenario: An analysis reveals that a specific city zone has an unusually high rate of delinquent auto loans. Further investigation attributes this to recent layoffs at a major employer in the area. Based on this insight, the bank decides to offer customized repayment plans and deploys additional field agents to the zone to improve engagement with affected customers.

Combining Route Optimization and Regional Analysis

When integrated, route optimization and regional analysis offer a powerful synergy for collections:

- **Efficient Field Deployment**: Regional analysis identifies high-risk zones, while route optimization ensures agents cover those zones efficiently.

- **Cost-Effective Operations**: By focusing on high-risk areas and optimizing travel routes, the bank minimizes expenses while maximizing recoveries.

- **Dynamic Adjustments**: If regional data shows a sudden spike in delinquencies in a particular area, the route optimization system can instantly reallocate resources to address the emerging risk.

In conclusion, **route optimization** and **regional analysis** are indispensable tools for improving the efficiency and effectiveness of field collections. By leveraging these analytics-driven strategies, banks and NBFCs can significantly enhance their operational outcomes and recovery rates.

Key Variables

1. **Travel Time Metrics:** Average time spent per field visit.

2. **Regional Risk Scores:** Delinquency patterns in specific areas.

3. **Resource Allocation:** Number of agents per region.

14.8 Compliance Analytics

Ensures that all collection activities are ethical and legally compliant.

Detailed Use Cases for Monitoring Communication and Legal Adherence in Collections

1. Monitoring Communication: Ensuring Adherence to Regulatory Norms

Monitoring communication is critical in collections to ensure that all customer interactions comply with regulatory guidelines and maintain ethical standards. This involves tracking and analysing communication between the bank's representatives (call center agents, field executives, and automated systems) and customers to prevent legal risks and reputational damage.

Key Aspects of Monitoring Communication:

- **Call Monitoring and Recording**: Records calls for quality assurance and regulatory compliance, ensuring agents follow approved scripts and protocols.

- **AI-Powered Speech Analytics**: Uses natural language processing (NLP) to detect compliance issues such as the use of inappropriate language, coercion, or threats during conversations.

- **Regulatory Checklist**: Ensures that all required disclosures, such as the overdue amount, payment due date, and consequences of non-payment, are communicated clearly to customers.

- **Digital Channel Monitoring**: Tracks communication via SMS, emails, chatbots, and voice bots to ensure that messages are accurate, non-misleading, and sent at permissible times.

- **Customer Feedback Mechanism**: Collects customer feedback on interactions to identify gaps in compliance and service quality.

Benefits:

- **Regulatory Compliance**: Prevents penalties and legal action by ensuring all interactions meet industry regulations and guidelines (e.g., Fair Debt Collection Practices Act or local laws).

- **Customer Trust**: Builds confidence in the bank by ensuring ethical communication practices.

- **Quality Assurance**: Helps identify training needs for agents to improve communication standards.

- **Proactive Risk Mitigation**: Detects compliance issues early, reducing the likelihood of disputes or complaints.

Example Scenario: A speech analytics tool flags a conversation where an agent failed to disclose the exact overdue amount during a collection call. The system triggers an alert, prompting the supervisor to coach the agent and ensure compliance in future calls.

2. Legal Adherence: Validating Repossession and Legal Processes

Legal adherence ensures that all repossession and legal actions are conducted in compliance with applicable laws and regulations. This safeguards the bank from legal disputes and protects the rights of customers.

Key Aspects of Legal Adherence:

- **Document Verification**: Ensures all necessary documents, such as loan agreements, demand notices, and payment histories, are in order before initiating legal action or repossession.

- **Regulatory Checkpoints**: Confirms adherence to legal frameworks like the SARFAESI Act (India), FDCPA (USA), or equivalent local laws.

- **Notice Management**: Tracks the issuance and delivery of mandatory notices to customers before repossession or legal action, such as 60-day demand notices under SARFAESI.

- **Court Order Validation**: Ensures that repossession actions requiring court approval are backed by valid orders.

- **Audit Trails**: Maintains detailed records of all actions taken during repossession and legal proceedings to provide evidence of compliance if challenged.

- **Legal Team Integration**: Involves the bank's legal department in high-stakes cases to ensure that all actions align with legal standards and mitigate risks.

Benefits:

- **Minimized Legal Risks**: Ensures repossession and legal actions are defensible in court, reducing the likelihood of adverse judgments or penalties.

- **Customer Protection**: Demonstrates the bank's commitment to ethical practices by respecting customer rights.

- **Enhanced Credibility**: Upholds the bank's reputation by avoiding negative publicity associated with unlawful or unethical repossession practices.

- **Efficient Legal Processes**: Streamlines legal workflows by automating compliance checks and approvals.

Example Scenario: Before repossessing a vehicle under the SARFAESI Act, a compliance system verifies that a demand notice was issued 60 days prior and acknowledges receipt by the customer. The repossession team then proceeds, ensuring the process adheres to the legal framework.

Integration of Monitoring Communication and Legal Adherence

The combination of these use cases ensures a robust and compliant collections process.

- **Real-Time Alerts**: If an agent communicates misleading information about repossession timelines, the system flags the issue, preventing legal risks.

- **Audit-Ready Processes**: Monitoring communication records and maintaining legal documentation create a seamless audit trail for regulatory checks.

- **Enhanced Customer Experience**: Ethical communication and legally sound processes reinforce customer confidence, even during challenging interactions like repossession.

By prioritizing **monitoring communication** and **legal adherence**, banks can balance their recovery goals with compliance and ethical responsibilities, fostering sustainable relationships with customers.

Key Variables

1. **Frequency of Calls:** Avoiding excessive reminders.

2. **Complaint Monitoring:** Tracking customer grievances.

3. **Regulatory Guidelines:** Ensuring process compliance.

Integrating these analytics into collections processes empowers financial institutions to make informed decisions, optimize resources, and maintain customer trust. Each analytics dimension provides a layer of insight that contributes to overall efficiency and recovery success.

15

The Role of Technology in Collections

In the current financial landscape, technology has become a crucial enabler in optimizing collections. From reducing manual interventions to providing personalized customer experiences, technology enhances operational efficiency, improves customer interactions, and ultimately drives better recovery rates. This section explores the many ways technology impacts collections, focusing on **Automation in Collections**, **AI and ML for Predictive Collections**, **Digital Payments and Collections**, and **Advanced Communication Channels like Voice Bots and Chatbots through WhatsApp**.

15.1 Automation with Chatbots, IVR, and Beyond

Automation in collections refers to the use of digital tools and systems to carry out repetitive tasks, allowing collections teams to focus on higher-value activities. Technologies like **Chatbots**, **IVR (Interactive Voice Response)**, and **RPA (Robotic Process Automation)** are driving this transformation.

Detailed Points:

Chatbots for Customer Interaction:

- **24/7 Availability**: Chatbots provide uninterrupted service, addressing customer inquiries such as payment reminders, missed EMIs, and other queries any time of the day.

- **Handling Routine Queries**: Chatbots efficiently handle frequent questions regarding payment due dates, loan balances, and payment methods, reducing the workload of human agents.

- **Proactive Payment Reminders**: Automated, personalized reminders ensure timely notifications for payments, reducing delinquency rates.

- **Escalation to Human Agents**: Chatbots can seamlessly hand over unresolved issues or complex queries to human agents, maintaining customer satisfaction.

- **Automated Negotiation for Payment Plans**: Bots can suggest payment plans or negotiate extensions based on predefined rules, streamlining the process for overdue accounts.

Voice Bots for Enhanced Communication:

- **Interactive Conversations**: Voice bots interact with customers via natural language, offering a human-like conversational experience.

- **Payment Assistance**: Customers can make payments directly through voice prompts, enhancing convenience.

- **Language Support**: Multilingual capabilities ensure effective communication with diverse customer bases.

- **Real-Time Data Updates**: Voice bots provide instant account updates, ensuring transparency in collections.

Chatbots Through WhatsApp:

- **Familiar Interface**: Leveraging WhatsApp's user-friendly platform enhances customer engagement.

- **Payment Links**: Bots can share clickable payment links, enabling quick transactions.

- **Rich Media Support**: Share documents like invoices or reminders through PDFs, improving communication clarity.

- **Two-Way Communication**: Allows customers to respond, request extensions, or seek clarification, making the process interactive and efficient.

IVR for Efficient Call Routing:

- **Self-Service Payments**: Customers can make payments via IVR without waiting for an agent.

- **Automated Reminders**: IVR systems send pre-recorded messages to remind customers of dues.

- **Personalized Messaging**: Tailored prompts based on customer data improve engagement.

- **Call Routing**: Routes calls to the right agents based on customer requirements, reducing resolution time.

RPA (Robotic Process Automation):

Detailed Use Case: Automating Repetitive Tasks with RPA

Robotic Process Automation (RPA) revolutionizes repetitive manual processes by automating routine, high-volume tasks. This ensures efficiency, reduces errors, and allows collections teams to focus on strategic activities like customer engagement or high-priority cases.

Automating Repetitive Tasks:

1. **Generating Payment Notices:**

   - **Dynamic Template Population:** RPA tools can populate pre-defined templates with customer-specific details (e.g., name, overdue amount, due dates) using data extracted from CRM or core banking systems.

   - **High-Volume Processing:** RPA handles bulk generation of payment notices for thousands of customers simultaneously, reducing turnaround time.

   - **Language Customization:** Notices can be generated in multiple languages based on the customer's preference, enhancing personalization.

2. **Updating Records:**

   - **Real-Time Updates:** RPA bots sync payment statuses from digital payment platforms or customer interactions and update core systems, ensuring real-time data accuracy.

   - **Error-Free Execution:** By automating data entry, RPA eliminates human errors, such as incorrect account updates or duplications.

- **Cross-System Integration:** Bots facilitate seamless data exchange between disparate systems (e.g., CRM, ERP, and payment gateways), ensuring uniformity across platforms.

3. Sending Reminders:

- **Scheduled Notifications:** RPA can schedule and send reminders via SMS, email, WhatsApp, or push notifications based on customer preferences or delinquency stage.

- **Personalized Messaging:** Bots customize the message content to include customer-specific details like overdue amounts, due dates, and penalty information.

- **Escalation Handling:** For accounts with no response, RPA escalates reminders to include stronger language or additional urgency triggers.

Benefits of Automating Repetitive Tasks with RPA:

- **Operational Efficiency:** Frees up human agents for complex tasks, reducing workload and speeding up collections processes.

- **Scalability:** Handles surges in account volumes (e.g., month-end delinquencies) without requiring additional staff.

- **Accuracy:** Eliminates errors common in manual data entry and communication.

- **Cost Savings:** Reduces reliance on human resources for repetitive tasks, cutting operational costs significantly.

Detailed Use Case: Document Automation with RPA

Document automation with RPA streamlines the creation, customization, and distribution of essential documents, ensuring timely communication and legal compliance.

1. Generating Key Documents:

Overdue Notices:

- **Automated Content Generation:** Bots pull customer details, overdue amounts, and due dates from internal systems to create overdue notices in real time.

- **Dynamic Formatting:** Ensures that each notice adheres to specific formats, regulatory guidelines, and organizational branding.

- **Multi-Channel Delivery:** Documents can be automatically sent via email, SMS (as links), or uploaded to customer portals for instant access.

Legal Letters:

- **Compliance-Driven Content:** Bots generate letters compliant with legal requirements (e.g., repossession notices or demand letters) using pre-approved templates.

- **Auto-Attachment of Supporting Documents:** Relevant attachments, such as payment schedules or account summaries, are included automatically.

- **Custom Scheduling:** Ensures that notices are sent within the stipulated timelines as per legal frameworks.

2. Distributing Documents:

Mass Distribution:

- RPA ensures simultaneous delivery of documents to multiple recipients, significantly reducing distribution delays.

Preferred Channels:

- Bots choose the customer's preferred communication channel (e.g., email, postal service, WhatsApp) based on predefined preferences in the system.

Tracking and Proof of Delivery:

- RPA integrates with tracking systems to confirm delivery status and logs these for compliance or future reference.

Benefits of Document Automation with RPA:

- **Timeliness:** Ensures documents are generated and sent immediately, avoiding delays that could impact collections outcomes.

- **Compliance Assurance:** Reduces the risk of non-compliance by adhering to regulatory requirements in both content and timelines.

- **Consistency:** Standardized templates ensure uniform communication across all accounts.

- **Auditability:** Logs all document generation and distribution activities, simplifying audits and dispute resolution.

By automating repetitive tasks and document generation, RPA not only enhances efficiency and accuracy but also ensures a professional, compliant, and customer-centric approach to collections.

15.2   AI and ML for Predictive Collections

AI and ML are revolutionizing collections by enabling data-driven decision-making, optimizing strategies, and predicting customer behaviour.

Detailed Use Case: Predictive Analytics for Risk Assessment

Predictive analytics leverages advanced statistical models, AI, and machine learning algorithms to analyse historical and real-time data, helping financial institutions identify risk patterns, anticipate defaults, and take proactive measures. Below is a detailed breakdown of its applications:

1. Risk Profiling:

Predictive analytics combines multiple data points to build comprehensive risk profiles for each customer, ensuring accurate segmentation and prioritization.

- **Customer Behaviour Analysis:** Analyses transactional data, spending patterns, and repayment tendencies to assess financial health and identify anomalies. For instance, customers who suddenly reduce spending or delay payments may indicate financial distress.

- **Payment History:** Examines historical data, such as timely payments, partial payments, or skipped payments, to assign risk scores. Customers with erratic payment behaviour are flagged as high risk.

- **Credit Scores:** Integrates external credit bureau scores with internal data to refine risk assessments. Lower scores or sudden declines may indicate increasing default risk.

- **Demographic and Psychographic Data:** Evaluates demographic factors (e.g., age, location, occupation) and psychographics (e.g., attitudes toward debt, financial discipline) to predict repayment likelihood.

Use Case: High-risk accounts are prioritized for early interventions, such as personalized payment plans or frequent follow-ups.

2. Anticipating Delinquencies: Machine learning models predict the likelihood of delinquency by analysing patterns in customer interactions and payments.

- **Pattern Recognition:** Identifies trends in customer payment behaviour, such as consistent late payments, gradual payment reductions, or skipped EMIs.

- **Delinquency Probability Scoring:** Assigns a probability score to each account based on predictive models, highlighting customers who are likely to miss upcoming payments.

- **Trigger Events Detection:** Flags trigger events, such as a customer requesting extensions, frequently changing contact details, or disputes over charges, which often precede delinquency.

Use Case: Accounts predicted to become delinquent are targeted with reminders, counselling, or alternate repayment options before they miss a payment.

3. Behavioural Insights:

Predictive analytics provides a deep understanding of customer behaviour, allowing institutions to tailor their engagement strategies effectively.

- **Payment Habit Monitoring:** Tracks payment consistency (e.g., frequency, amount, mode) to identify deviations from usual patterns, such as paying less than the usual instalment amount.

- **Financial Lifecycle Mapping:** Maps a customer's financial lifecycle (e.g., income inflow dates, seasonal fluctuations in earnings) to predict repayment capacity and schedule follow-ups accordingly.

- **Engagement Insights:** Analyses how customers respond to past collection efforts (e.g., email open rates, call responses) to identify the best channels and timings for outreach.

Use Case: Customers showing a dip in consistent payments can receive targeted communication, such as reminders or educational resources, to encourage timely repayment.

4. Early Warnings:

Predictive analytics acts as an early warning system by flagging accounts showing signs of financial stress or deteriorating risk profiles.

- **Deterioration Indicators:** Monitors indicators like missed payments, reduced transaction activity, or increased credit utilization to detect potential financial instability.

- **Dynamic Risk Scoring:** Continuously updates risk scores based on real-time data, ensuring immediate identification of worsening profiles.

- **Proactive Alerts:** Generates automated alerts for collections teams when certain thresholds are crossed (e.g., two consecutive missed payments or a drop in credit score), enabling immediate follow-up.

Use Case: Early warnings enable collections teams to contact customers and offer solutions, such as deferments or counselling, before the situation escalates.

Benefits of Predictive Analytics in Risk Assessment:

1. **Proactive Intervention:** Enables early action, reducing the likelihood of defaults.

2. **Targeted Resource Allocation:** Focuses collections efforts on high-risk accounts, maximizing efficiency.

3. **Improved Recovery Rates:** Early detection and personalized strategies enhance repayment outcomes.

4. **Enhanced Customer Experience:** Tailored outreach based on behavioural insights ensures respectful and effective communication.

By leveraging predictive analytics, financial institutions can turn collections into a proactive, customer-focused process, minimizing defaults while maintaining positive customer relationships.

Personalized Collection Strategies:

- **Tailored Payment Plans**: Suggests repayment options based on financial history and capacity.

- **Optimized Communication Channels**: Determines the most effective methods to contact customers.

- **Segmented Outreach**: Focuses on specific customer groups (e.g., frequent defaulters) for targeted efforts.

Customer Segmentation and Prioritization:

- **Risk-Based Segmentation**: Prioritizes accounts based on default likelihood.

- **Behavioural Grouping**: Groups customers by responsiveness or payment patterns for tailored strategies.

15.3   Digital Payments and Collections: Reducing Friction

Digital payment platforms have streamlined collections, offering customers convenient and secure payment options.

Detailed Use Case: Multiple Payment Channels

Offering diverse payment channels allows customers to choose the most convenient option, improving payment compliance, reducing friction, and increasing recovery rates. Below is a detailed explanation of key payment channels and their role in collections:

1. Online Banking and UPI: Facilitates Real-Time Transactions

Online banking and Unified Payments Interface (UPI) systems provide customers with secure and instant payment methods.

- **Real-Time Processing:** Payments are processed instantly, and the updates reflect immediately in the lender's system, reducing delays in crediting funds. This is especially useful for last-minute or overdue payments.

- **Ease of Access:** Customers can pay directly from their bank accounts without needing to visit a branch or ATM. This reduces inconvenience and encourages timely payments.

- **24/7 Availability:** These channels are accessible round-the-clock, ensuring customers can make payments at their convenience, even outside working hours.

- **Low Transaction Costs:** UPI transactions are generally free or low-cost, providing an economical option for customers and financial institutions.

Use Case: A customer receiving a payment reminder can instantly transfer funds via UPI to clear their dues, avoiding penalties and maintaining a positive relationship with the lender.

2. Mobile Wallets: Seamless Payments Through Apps Like Paytm or Google Pay

Mobile wallets have become a preferred payment method due to their ease of use and widespread adoption.

- **User-Friendly Interface:** Apps like Paytm, Google Pay, and PhonePe offer intuitive interfaces, allowing customers to complete transactions with a few clicks.

- **Integrated Features:** Wallets often come with features like bill splitting, payment reminders, and transaction history, helping customers manage their payments efficiently.

- **Instant Receipts:** Customers receive immediate confirmation of successful transactions, reducing disputes and enhancing trust.

- **Widespread Adoption:** Mobile wallets are especially popular in emerging markets, where smartphone penetration is high but access to traditional banking services may be limited.

Use Case: A customer overdue on an EMI can use Google Pay to settle their account in seconds, without needing to log into a bank portal or carry physical cash.

3. Payment Links: Quick Access to Payment Options via SMS, Email, or WhatsApp

Payment links simplify the payment process by providing direct access to payment gateways.

- **Ease of Use:** Customers receive a clickable link that directs them to a secure payment page where they can choose their preferred payment method.

- **Omni-Channel Reach:** Links can be sent via SMS, email, or instant messaging platforms like WhatsApp, ensuring customers receive reminders on their most-used communication channels.

- **No Login Required:** Unlike traditional banking apps, payment links do not require customers to log into their accounts, making the process faster and more convenient.

- **Customizable Options:** Links can be pre-configured with customer details (e.g., loan number, amount due), minimizing errors and ensuring seamless payment.

Use Case: A collections agent sends a payment link to a customer via WhatsApp. The customer clicks the link, selects a payment method (e.g., UPI or card), and completes the transaction within minutes.

Benefits of Multiple Payment Channels

1. **Convenience for Customers:** Providing a variety of channels allows customers to choose the one that best suits their preferences and circumstances.

2. **Faster Recovery:** Instant payment options ensure quicker credit of funds, improving cash flow for the lender.

3. **Wider Accessibility:** Channels like UPI and mobile wallets make it easier to reach customers in remote areas or those with limited access to traditional banking.

4. **Reduced Friction:** Simplified payment processes (e.g., one-click links) minimize barriers to payment, improving customer compliance.

5. **Enhanced Customer Experience:** Offering multiple options shows flexibility and consideration, building customer trust and satisfaction.

By integrating these channels, financial institutions can significantly improve the efficiency and effectiveness of their collections processes while meeting the evolving expectations of digitally-savvy customers.

Real-Time Payments:

- **Instant Updates**: Transactions reflect immediately in customer accounts.

- **Payment Confirmations**: Real-time alerts reassure customers and reduce disputes.

Recurring Payment Options:

- **Auto Debit**: Automates payments, reducing defaults.

- **Flexible Dates**: Customers can choose payment dates aligned with their income cycle.

The integration of advanced automation, predictive analytics, and digital payment platforms is transforming collections into a more efficient, customer-centric process. Tools like **Voice Bots** and **Chatbots through WhatsApp** further enhance accessibility and convenience, ensuring better engagement and recovery rates. As financial institutions continue adopting these technologies, collections will evolve to be more strategic, ethical, and results-driven, benefitting both lenders and customers.

16

The Role of Cross-Functional Collaboration in Collections

Cross-functional collaboration plays a critical role in ensuring the effectiveness of collections processes in financial institutions. By integrating the expertise of various teams, collections departments can optimize their strategies, address complex issues, and enhance overall portfolio quality. This section explores how partnerships with key departments, such as Customer Service, Legal, Residual Management, and Insurance, along with governance models, contribute to efficient collections.

16.1   Customer Service Collaboration

Effective collaboration between customer service and collections teams is pivotal in enhancing the overall efficiency of collections processes. Customer service teams play a vital role in establishing a positive first line of interaction with borrowers, ensuring early identification of potential issues and seamless transitions into recovery actions when needed.

1. Proactive Customer Engagement

Customer service teams often act as the first point of contact for borrowers facing challenges. By maintaining open communication, they can detect early signs of financial distress, such as delayed payments or inquiries about payment plans.

- **Early Issue Detection:** Borrowers having trouble often approach customer service to discuss concerns, such as job loss, medical expenses, or temporary cash flow problems.

- **Problem-Solving Role:** By providing guidance on options such as payment extensions or restructuring, customer service agents can reduce the risk of borrowers defaulting.

- **Building Trust:** Empathetic and proactive communication helps strengthen the borrower's relationship with the financial institution, making them more likely to cooperate during tough times.

Example:

A borrower calls customer service to discuss concerns about meeting an upcoming EMI due to unexpected medical expenses. The agent identifies this as a potential early warning signal and flags the account for follow-up by the collections team.

2. Customer Retention

Empathetic handling of borrower concerns by customer service teams can significantly reduce the likelihood of defaults while preserving customer relationships.

- **De-escalation of Issues:** When borrowers feel heard and supported, they are more likely to cooperate and work towards resolution.

- **Customized Solutions:** Customer service teams can suggest tailored solutions, such as adjusted repayment schedules or temporary deferrals, to help borrowers navigate financial difficulties without defaulting.

- **Retention Through Support:** By addressing issues promptly and empathetically, institutions can retain borrowers, ensuring they stay within the ecosystem and continue to be viable long-term customers.

Example:

A borrower nearing delinquency contacts customer service to discuss restructuring their loan. The agent collaborates with collections to offer a solution that includes reduced EMIs for six months, enabling the borrower to recover financially while maintaining their loan obligations.

3. Seamless Handover

For cases requiring specialized intervention, smooth coordination between customer service and collections teams is essential to ensure continuity and maintain a positive customer experience.

- **Clear Escalation Protocols:** Customer service teams must be equipped with clear guidelines for escalating cases to collections, ensuring timely intervention.

- **Shared Systems and Tools:** Utilizing integrated CRM systems allows both teams to access up-to-date borrower information, reducing redundancies and miscommunication.

- **Maintaining Service Quality:** Even when transitioning a case to collections, the borrower should feel supported and valued, rather than stigmatized or pressured.

Example:

A borrower struggling to make payments calls customer service to request assistance. The agent listens to the concerns, updates the borrower's profile, and escalates the case to collections. The collections team reviews the borrower's history and offers a personalized payment plan, ensuring a smooth transition without disrupting the customer experience.

Use Case

A borrower contacts customer service, expressing difficulty in making upcoming EMI payments due to unexpected financial challenges.

1. The customer service agent empathetically listens to the borrower, offering reassurance and outlining available options.

2. Recognizing the need for specialized intervention, the agent escalates the case to the collections team.

3. The collections team reviews the borrower's payment history and financial situation.

4. A customized payment plan is proposed, such as reduced EMIs for three months, with the assurance of revisiting the case afterward.

5. The borrower accepts the plan, avoids delinquency, and retains a positive view of the institution.

Key Benefits of Customer Service Collaboration in Collections

1. **Early Intervention:** Proactively identifying issues reduces the likelihood of accounts becoming delinquent.

2. **Improved Customer Experience:** Borrowers feel supported, increasing their willingness to cooperate.

3. **Higher Retention Rates:** Empathetic handling and tailored solutions help retain borrowers as long-term customers.

4. **Operational Efficiency:** Clear protocols and seamless handovers ensure smooth transitions between teams.

By fostering strong collaboration between customer service and collections teams, financial institutions can create a borrower-centric approach that not only improves recovery rates but also strengthens customer loyalty and trust.

16.2   Legal Team Collaboration

Collaboration between collections teams and legal departments is critical to ensure adherence to regulatory frameworks and to effectively handle high-risk or non-cooperative accounts. Legal teams provide the necessary expertise to navigate complex regulations, initiate legal proceedings when required, and ensure that all documentation and processes are accurate and enforceable.

1. Compliance Assurance

Legal teams play a pivotal role in ensuring that the collections process adheres to local laws, industry regulations, and ethical guidelines. Non-compliance can lead to significant legal and reputational risks.

- **Regulatory Adherence:** Legal teams provide guidance on debt collection practices that align with consumer protection laws, such as fair debt collection practices acts and data privacy regulations.

- **Safeguarding Against Lawsuits:** By reviewing collection scripts, notices, and procedures, legal teams minimize the risk of borrower lawsuits or regulatory penalties.

- **Ethical Oversight:** Legal teams ensure that the collections process is conducted ethically and fairly, avoiding harassment or coercion, which could harm the institution's reputation.

Example:

Before launching a new collections campaign, the legal team reviews all communication templates to ensure they comply with local debt recovery laws, preventing potential legal disputes.

2. Legal Interventions

When traditional collection efforts fail, legal teams step in to initiate legal proceedings or provide strategic advice on next steps, ensuring the organization's interests are protected.

- **Guidance on Repossessions:** Legal teams advise on the initiation of repossession proceedings for secured loans, ensuring compliance with local repossession laws and minimizing the risk of disputes.

- **Arbitration and Litigation:** For non-cooperative accounts, legal teams evaluate whether arbitration, mediation, or litigation is the most effective course of action, considering costs and likelihood of recovery.

- **Handling Complex Cases:** Legal experts address cases involving disputes, bankruptcy filings, or other legal complications, ensuring that the institution's recovery efforts remain within legal boundaries.

Example:

A borrower with a secured loan defaults and refuses to pay despite repeated attempts by the collections team. The legal team intervenes, reviews the loan agreement, and advises repossession of the pledged collateral through court-approved procedures.

3. Documentation Support

Accurate and enforceable documentation is vital in collections, particularly when escalating cases to legal action. Legal teams ensure that all notices, contracts, and case files meet legal standards.

- **Preparation of Legal Notices:** Legal teams draft and validate notices of default, demand letters, and repossession warnings to ensure they comply with statutory requirements.

- **Case File Validation:** Before initiating legal proceedings, legal teams review case files to confirm that all necessary documentation, such as loan agreements, payment records, and correspondence logs, is complete and accurate.

- **Contract Review:** Legal teams assess the enforceability of loan agreements and other contracts, ensuring that the institution's claims are well-founded in court or arbitration.

Example:

The collections team prepares a default notice for a borrower who has missed multiple payments. The legal team reviews the notice, ensuring it adheres to local regulations and includes all necessary details, such as the overdue amount and consequences of non-payment.

Use Case

A borrower repeatedly ignores payment reminders and refuses to negotiate or cooperate with the collections team.

1. The collections team escalates the case to the legal department after exhausting all standard recovery efforts.

2. The legal team reviews the borrower's account, including loan agreements and payment history, to confirm grounds for legal action.

3. A notice of default is issued, warning the borrower of impending legal proceedings if payment is not made within a specified period.

4. When the borrower remains non-compliant, the legal team initiates repossession proceedings for secured

assets, ensuring all actions comply with local laws and are documented thoroughly.

5. The institution recovers the collateral, minimizing financial losses while maintaining legal and ethical integrity.

Key Benefits of Legal Team Collaboration in Collections

1. **Mitigating Legal Risks:** Ensures collections processes comply with regulations, reducing exposure to lawsuits and penalties.

2. **Efficient Escalations:** Provides a structured pathway for handling high-risk or non-cooperative accounts, enhancing recovery rates.

3. **Accurate Documentation:** Legal oversight ensures that all notices, contracts, and case files are accurate and enforceable.

4. **Reputation Protection:** By adhering to legal and ethical standards, the institution safeguards its brand image and avoids negative publicity.

5. **Strategic Decision-Making:** Legal teams provide valuable advice on the best course of action for complex cases, balancing costs, and recovery potential.

By fostering close collaboration with legal teams, collections departments can operate with greater confidence, knowing that their processes are legally sound and strategically effective. This partnership is integral to maintaining compliance, protecting the institution's reputation, and optimizing recovery efforts.

16.3   Residual Management Team Collaboration

Residual management plays a vital role in the collections process, particularly in cases involving secured loans backed by physical assets. By collaborating closely with the collections team, the residual management team ensures that repossessed or returned assets are handled strategically to minimize losses and maximize recovery. Their expertise in asset valuation, disposal, and reallocation significantly enhances the effectiveness of recovery strategies.

1. Asset Valuation

The residual management team evaluates the current market value of repossessed or returned assets, providing critical data for decision-making.

- **Accurate Pricing:** By conducting detailed market research and inspections, the team determines the fair market value of the asset, which serves as a baseline for recovery efforts.

- **Informed Recovery Strategies:** Accurate asset valuation helps the collections team decide whether to pursue refurbishment, resale, or auction, ensuring the most profitable approach.

- **Depreciation Analysis:** For assets like vehicles or machinery, the residual team considers depreciation and market trends to estimate potential recovery value.

Example:

A repossessed vehicle is appraised by the residual management team, which identifies its current market value based on condition, mileage, and market demand. This valuation guides the strategy for its disposal.

2. Optimal Disposal

The residual management team identifies the most effective channels for liquidating assets, ensuring maximum recovery.

- **Auctioning Assets:** Organizing public or private auctions to sell repossessed items quickly while achieving competitive prices.

- **Direct Sales:** Collaborating with authorized dealers or buyers for direct asset sales, often yielding higher recovery amounts compared to auctions.

- **Market Timing:** Recommending the best time to sell an asset based on market trends, avoiding losses due to seasonal or economic fluctuations.

Example:

A repossessed piece of construction equipment is sold through a specialized auction platform for heavy machinery, enabling the institution to recover a substantial portion of the outstanding debt.

3. Reallocation / Refurbishment of Assets Strategies

Residual management teams explore ways to reallocate or refurbish assets to enhance their value before sale, reducing financial losses.

- **Refurbishment and Repair:** For assets like vehicles or machinery, minor repairs and maintenance can significantly increase their resale value.

- **Reusing Assets Internally:** In some cases, assets may be repurposed for internal use, such as using repossessed equipment within the organization, reducing the need for new purchases.

- **Bulk Liquidation:** Collaborating with dealers to sell multiple repossessed assets in bulk, often at negotiated prices that maximize overall recovery.

Example:

A repossessed vehicle is refurbished by the residual management team with minor repairs and cosmetic enhancements. It is then sold at a higher price through a certified pre-owned vehicle program, recovering a significant portion of the loan balance.

Use Case: Repossessed Vehicle Recovery and Disposal

1. A borrower defaults on a vehicle loan, and the car is repossessed by the collections team.

2. The vehicle is handed over to the residual management team for assessment.

3. The team evaluates its condition, appraises its current market value, and recommends refurbishment to enhance resale potential.

4. After refurbishment, the vehicle is listed for auction.

5. The sale generates a substantial recovery amount, reducing the financial impact of the borrower's default.

Key Benefits of Residual Management Collaboration

1. **Maximized Recovery:** Expert valuation and optimized disposal strategies ensure that repossessed assets yield the highest possible returns.

2. **Informed Decisions:** Accurate asset appraisals enable the collections team to adopt the most effective recovery strategies.

3. **Reduced Losses:** Refurbishment and strategic reallocation minimize financial losses associated with asset depreciation.

4. **Efficient Asset Handling:** Residual management ensures that repossessed assets are processed, sold, or repurposed quickly, avoiding storage costs or further depreciation.

5. **Strategic Market Insights:** The team's knowledge of market trends and buyer behaviour enhances the institution's ability to recover debts effectively.

By integrating the expertise of residual management into the collections process, financial institutions can turn repossessed assets into valuable recovery opportunities. This collaboration strengthens the institution's overall recovery framework, ensuring a more sustainable approach to managing default scenarios.

16.4   The Synergy Between Collections & Insurance

The collaboration between collections and insurance teams creates a powerful synergy, allowing financial institutions to mitigate risks, recover funds, and enhance customer experiences. This partnership leverages insurance as a risk mitigation tool while enabling integrated strategies for risk assessment and customer engagement.

1. Insurance as a Risk Mitigation Tool

a. Claim Processing for Defaulted Loans

Insurance teams play a critical role in recovering funds through claims on credit protection plans or loan insurance policies.

- **Coverage Activation:** When a borrower defaults due to unforeseen circumstances such as death, disability, or job loss, insurance teams activate policies to cover the outstanding loan amount.

- **Streamlined Processes:** A well-coordinated approach ensures quick claim processing, minimizing delays in fund recovery.

- **Financial Stability:** This mechanism protects financial institutions from incurring significant losses while alleviating financial stress on borrowers' families.

Example:

A borrower with loan protection insurance passes away unexpectedly. The insurance team efficiently processes the claim, ensuring the lender recovers the outstanding loan amount without placing any financial burden on the borrower's family.

b. **Minimizing Losses**

Insurance policies act as a safety net for financial institutions, allowing them to recover funds that might otherwise be unrecoverable.

- **Loan Coverage Policies:** Institutions can recover significant portions of outstanding amounts in cases of default or other covered events.

- **Default Mitigation:** Insurance mitigates risks associated with high-value or long-tenure loans, reducing the financial impact of defaults.

Example:

A borrower who loses their job is unable to make payments. The insurance team processes the claim under a job-loss protection policy, covering the loan payments until the borrower regains employment.

c. **Risk Segmentation Support**

Insurance data contributes valuable insights for better risk profiling and segmentation.

- **Pattern Identification:** By analysing data on insured versus uninsured borrowers, financial institutions can identify trends and behaviours that correlate with lower risks.

- **Targeted Strategies:** Institutions can focus risk mitigation efforts on segments with higher default probabilities, optimizing resource allocation.

Example:

Data analysis reveals that insured borrowers have a lower default rate. The collections team uses this insight to target uninsured borrowers with customized recovery strategies.

2. Integrated Risk Assessment

a. **Coordinated Risk Evaluation**

Collaboration between insurance and collections teams facilitates a comprehensive risk evaluation process.

- **Data Sharing:** Combining insights from insurance policies and collections activities helps identify vulnerabilities in borrower profiles.

- **Predictive Models:** Shared data enhances predictive analytics, enabling proactive strategies to mitigate risks before defaults occur.

Example:

The collections team identifies a borrower struggling with payments. Coordinating with the insurance team, they discover the borrower has no loan protection. This information guides the collections strategy to propose viable solutions.

b. **Policy Selling During Recovery**

Insurance teams can support collections efforts by offering relevant policies to borrowers during the recovery process.

- **Proactive Engagement:** Suggesting credit protection insurance or other risk mitigation products during conversations with borrowers enhances financial security.

- **Future Risk Mitigation:** Policies offered at the right time reduce future risks for both borrowers and the institution.

Example:

A borrower nearing delinquency is contacted by collections. During the discussion, the insurance team proposes a credit protection policy. The borrower agrees, safeguarding future obligations and reducing potential risks.

Key Benefits of Collections and Insurance Collaboration

1. **Enhanced Risk Mitigation:** Insurance ensures that defaults due to unforeseen circumstances are less financially impactful.

2. **Improved Recovery Rates:** Claim processing provides an alternative recovery channel, reducing dependency on collections alone.

3. **Data-Driven Strategies:** Insights from insurance data refine risk segmentation, improving the effectiveness of collection strategies.

4. **Customer-Centric Solutions:** Offering insurance policies during recovery promotes financial stability for borrowers while protecting institutional interests.

5. **Streamlined Operations:** Coordinated efforts between the two teams improve efficiency in claims processing and risk assessment.

Use Case: Comprehensive Risk Mitigation

6. A borrower defaults due to a job loss.

7. The collections team identifies the default and consults the insurance team.

8. The insurance team processes the claim under a job-loss protection policy, covering the borrower's payments during unemployment.

9. During the recovery conversation, the borrower is also offered additional credit protection insurance, which they accept.

10. The lender recovers funds through the claim while reducing the risk of future defaults.

By integrating the efforts of collections and insurance teams, financial institutions create a robust framework for managing risks, recovering funds, and supporting borrowers effectively.

16.5 Governance Models to Streamline Collaboration

Governance models that facilitate collaboration across departments, such as collections, customer service, legal, and insurance, are essential for effective portfolio management. These models ensure seamless coordination, clear accountability, and optimal resource utilization.

1. Centralized Governance Models

a. Defined Roles and Responsibilities

- Clear demarcation of roles prevents confusion and overlaps, ensuring every team member knows their specific responsibilities.

- Accountability frameworks improve response times and decision-making in high-risk situations.

b. Data Sharing Protocols

- Establishing secure, standardized protocols for sharing customer and portfolio data fosters real-time, consistent insights.

- Ensures all teams access accurate and updated information for coordinated decision-making.

c. Central Command Structure

- A unified decision-making framework, such as a governance council, oversees cross-departmental collaboration.

- Helps prioritize high-risk cases, ensuring cohesive strategies rather than fragmented actions.

Use Case: A governance council comprising representatives from collections, legal, customer service, and insurance meets weekly to analyse delinquency trends. The council devises coordinated strategies for high-risk accounts, leveraging each team's expertise.

2. Process Integration

a. Standard Operating Procedures (SOPs)

- SOPs standardize workflows across teams, ensuring consistency in operations and efficient handovers.

- Clear guidelines facilitate smooth collaboration during recovery efforts, reducing delays.

b. Technology Enablement

- Shared platforms, such as Customer Relationship Management (CRM) systems, allow all teams to access unified customer histories, risk profiles, and task statuses.

- Eliminates duplication of effort and improves transparency.

Use Case: A shared CRM system alerts collections, legal, and customer service teams about updates to a delinquent account. This ensures coordinated and timely follow-up actions across departments, avoiding lapses or conflicting communications.

3. Performance Metrics and Feedback Loops

a. Joint KPIs

- Cross-functional teams adopt shared Key Performance Indicators (KPIs), such as recovery rates, resolution times, and customer satisfaction scores.

- Aligning goals fosters accountability and collaboration.

b. **Continuous Improvement**

- Regular feedback sessions between departments identify bottlenecks, enabling teams to refine processes.

- Encourages a culture of adaptability and proactive problem-solving.

Use Case: After identifying delays in legal escalations, the collections and legal teams introduce a shared escalation tracking system. This reduces turnaround times and improves recovery outcomes.

Key Benefits of Cross-Functional Collaboration

1. **Enhanced Efficiency:** Coordinated efforts eliminate redundancies, streamline workflows, and reduce operational costs.

2. **Comprehensive Risk Management:** Involvement of multiple teams ensures robust strategies for identifying and mitigating risks.

3. **Improved Recovery Rates:** Leveraging the expertise of legal, customer service, and insurance teams enhances the effectiveness of recovery strategies.

4. **Stronger Customer Relationships:** Seamless collaboration minimizes disruptions in customer interactions, preserving trust and satisfaction.

5. **Regulatory Compliance:** Close coordination with the legal team ensures adherence to regulations, safeguarding against penalties and reputational damage.

Conclusion

By implementing centralized governance models, integrating processes, and tracking shared performance metrics, financial institutions can foster a collaborative culture. This approach creates a robust collections framework that enhances operational efficiency, strengthens customer relationships, and ensures long-term portfolio health.

"Every contact counts in collections."

- **Background:** This principle is derived from industry insights, emphasizing that every interaction with a customer is an opportunity to recover dues or improve relationships. It is fundamental to field and digital collections strategies.

17

Field vs. Digital Collections

As financial institutions adapt to technological advancements and changing customer behaviours, collections processes are shifting from traditional field collections to digital-first strategies. However, certain situations still require the human touch, making field collections indispensable. This section explores the evolution of collections strategies, the opportunities and challenges of digital-first approaches, the enduring relevance of field collections, and the value of hybrid models.

17.1   The Shift to Digital-First Collections

As the financial industry evolves, organizations are embracing digital-first strategies to enhance operational efficiency and customer experience. This section explores the opportunities that digital-first collections offer and the challenges they present, along with strategies to overcome them.

Opportunities

1. Scalability

- **Engagement at Scale:** Digital-first strategies enable financial institutions to engage many customers simultaneously. Automated communication tools such as SMS, email campaigns, IVR systems, and mobile apps ensure that borrowers are reached promptly and consistently.

- **High-Volume Interaction Management:** Platforms like WhatsApp and web-based portals allow for efficient handling of high query volumes, reducing response times and eliminating bottlenecks in communication.

2. Cost Efficiency

- **Operational Cost Savings:** By automating repetitive tasks such as payment reminders, follow-ups, and account updates, organizations significantly reduce costs associated with manual processes and field agent operations.

- **Resource Optimization:** Minimizing reliance on field visits, logistics, and transportation helps reallocate resources toward strategic initiatives or high-priority cases.

3. Enhanced Customer Experience

- **24/7 Accessibility:** Borrowers value the convenience of self-service capabilities available around the clock, including payment processing, grievance resolution, and the selection of repayment plans.

- **Personalized Interactions:** Data-driven tools send tailored nudges, such as reminders aligned with a borrower's payment history or alerts for upcoming due dates, fostering trust and timely action.

4. Data-Driven Insights

- **Real-Time Monitoring:** Advanced analytics enable real-time tracking of customer behaviour, helping organizations identify risk signals and adjust strategies accordingly.

- **Segmented Engagement:** Digital tools categorize customers based on repayment patterns, risk profiles, and demographics, enabling targeted communication and intervention.

5. Compliance Management

- **Pre-Built Compliance:** Automated workflows are designed to align with regulatory frameworks, ensuring adherence to industry norms during communication and recovery.

- **Transparency:** Digital channels record every interaction, providing an auditable trail that protects organizations during disputes or regulatory checks.

Challenges

1. Digital Divide

- **Limited Access:** Borrowers in rural or economically disadvantaged areas may lack smartphones, stable internet connections, or the technical knowledge to utilize digital tools.

- **Adaptability Gaps:** Financial institutions must design alternative approaches to accommodate such demographics without losing effectiveness.

2. Impersonal Engagement

- **Lack of Human Touch:** Automated messages can lack the empathy required in sensitive or high-stress scenarios, such as when borrowers face financial difficulties.

- **Customer Perception:** High-value borrowers may feel neglected if digital interactions replace personalized service, potentially impacting loyalty and satisfaction.

3. Lower Effectiveness for Complex Cases

- **Limited Resolution Capabilities:** Complex issues, such as disputes over documentation errors or legal proceedings, require nuanced conversations and often exceed the scope of digital tools.

- **Escalation Needs:** Automated systems may not effectively identify cases requiring immediate manual intervention, leading to delays.

4. Resistance to Change

- **Borrower Hesitation:** Customers accustomed to traditional methods, such as in-person visits or branch interactions, may distrust digital tools or find them intimidating.

- **Adoption Barriers:** Institutions may face challenges in encouraging these customers to transition to digital channels.

Strategies to Overcome Challenges

1. Omnichannel Capabilities

- **Seamless Integration:** By combining digital and field-based strategies, institutions can offer borrowers a choice of channels that suit their needs. For instance, while chatbots address simple queries, complex cases can be escalated to human representatives or field visits.

2. Customer Training and Awareness

- **Educational Initiatives:** Borrowers unfamiliar with digital tools can benefit from in-app tutorials, SMS-based guides, or community workshops. These efforts are especially crucial in regions with low digital literacy.

Demonstrating Value: Highlighting the convenience and speed of digital channels through customer testimonials or case studies can encourage adoption.

3. User-Friendly Interfaces

- **Simplified Design:** Digital platforms should feature intuitive designs, multilingual support, and step-by-step guidance to ensure inclusivity.

- **Feedback Loops:** Regular updates and refinements based on user feedback help maintain a positive customer experience.

4. Behavioural Insights

- **Proactive Adjustments:** Analytics can identify scenarios where borrowers prefer personal engagement.

For example, early signals of distress may prompt a shift from digital channels to field visits or personal calls.

- **Personalization at Scale:** Incorporating behavioural insights into automated workflows ensures that even digital interactions feel tailored and relevant.

By understanding the opportunities and challenges of digital-first collections and implementing strategies to address potential barriers, financial institutions can maximize efficiency, enhance customer satisfaction, and build a future-ready collections framework.

17.2   Leveraging Field Collections

Field collections remain a vital component of a comprehensive collections strategy, especially in cases requiring personal engagement or intervention. This section highlights the significance of field collections, outlines best practices, and explains how they complement digital strategies.

Why Field Collections Matter

1. High-Value or Sensitive Cases

- **Building Trust and Rapport:** Personal visits allow field agents to engage directly with borrowers, fostering trust, particularly for loans with large outstanding balances or long-term delinquencies.

- **Customized Solutions:** Field interactions facilitate tailored repayment plans that address the borrower's unique financial circumstances.

2. Complex Disputes

- **Enhanced Communication:** In-person interactions help clarify misunderstandings, such as discrepancies in loan terms or payment records, and allow agents to explain terms in a more effective manner.

- **Negotiation Capabilities:** Field agents can mediate disputes and negotiate settlements, reducing the likelihood of prolonged delinquency or escalation to legal actions.

3. Emotional Support for Borrowers

- **Empathy in Action:** Borrowers experiencing financial hardship, such as job losses, medical emergencies, or natural disasters, may benefit from direct emotional reassurance and empathy provided by a field agent.

- **Relationship Strengthening:** Personal interactions signal that the institution values the borrower's situation, reinforcing trust and encouraging repayment.

4. Low-Digital Penetration Areas

- **Rural and Semi-Urban Outreach:** In regions with limited internet access or low digital literacy, field agents bridge the communication gap, ensuring consistent borrower engagement.

- **Localized Approach:** Field agents can adapt their communication and strategy to local cultural norms, further enhancing the effectiveness of outreach.

Best Practices for Field Collections

1. Comprehensive Agent Training

- **Skill Development:** Train field agents in critical skills, such as negotiation, active listening, and cultural sensitivity, to handle a diverse range of borrowers effectively.

- **Situational Awareness:** Educate agents about different borrower personas, potential objections, and strategies to de-escalate tense situations.

- **Ethical Practices:** Reinforce the importance of professionalism and ethical conduct during borrower interactions.

2. Digital Enablement

- **Real-Time Tools:** Equip agents with mobile apps or digital platforms to track repayment schedules, record interactions, and generate digital receipts on the spot for transparency.

- **Data Integration:** Field agents should have access to real-time borrower data to make informed decisions during interactions.

- **Efficiency Boosters:** Digital tools enable field agents to manage time and resources effectively, ensuring more productive visits.

3. Regulatory Compliance

- **Adherence to Local Laws:** Train field agents on the legal requirements governing borrower interactions, such as limitations on collection hours and permissible communication methods.

- **Documentation Standards:** Ensure agents log all interactions and agreements accurately to provide an auditable trail.

- **Risk Mitigation:** Monitoring compliance reduces the likelihood of legal disputes or reputational damage to the institution.

4. Integration with Digital Tools

- **Optimized Visit Scheduling:** Use predictive analytics and digital scheduling tools to prioritize visits based on risk level, account value, and borrower behaviour.

- **Performance Monitoring:** Track field agent activities and outcomes through centralized platforms, enabling data-driven insights and improvements.

- **Hybrid Collaboration:** Field collections should complement digital strategies, switching between field and digital engagement as the borrower's situation demands.

Key Takeaway

While digital strategies have revolutionized collections, field collections retain their importance in high-touch scenarios. Combining personal engagement with digital tools and best practices ensures that organizations can handle sensitive cases effectively while maintaining a borrower-centric approach.

17.3   Case Studies on Hybrid Collection Models

Hybrid collection models blend digital tools with field strategies to leverage the strengths of both approaches. These models are particularly effective in addressing diverse borrower profiles and geographical challenges. Below are two detailed case studies demonstrating their efficacy.

Case Study 1: Urban Loan Recovery – Digitally Driven with Field Support

Context

A financial institution catering to salaried urban professionals sought to optimize recovery from early delinquencies while minimizing operational costs.

Approach

1. **Automated Digital Engagement**

   - **Payment Reminders:** Automated SMS and email reminders were sent to borrowers, incorporating clickable payment links for instant transactions.

   - **Chatbots for Query Resolution:** AI-powered chatbots handled routine queries, such as outstanding balances, due dates, and repayment options, reducing the burden on customer service teams.

   - **Dynamic Repayment Plans:** Borrowers received personalized repayment plan suggestions based on their delinquency stage, encouraging faster resolutions.

2. **Escalation to Field Agents**

   o **Non-Responsive Borrowers:** High-value accounts or cases where borrowers failed to respond digitally were escalated to field agents for direct intervention.

   o **Field Support for Settlements:** Field agents offered face-to-face negotiations for settlements, tailored to the borrower's financial situation.

Outcome

- **Digital Success:** 70% of early delinquent accounts were resolved within 30 days through digital outreach alone, showcasing the efficiency of automated tools.

- **Field Intervention Impact:** Recovery rates for escalated cases improved by 15%, highlighting the critical role of field agents in complementing digital strategies.

- **Cost Savings:** The hybrid model reduced dependency on field operations for routine cases, lowering operational costs while ensuring high-value cases received personal attention.

Case Study 2: Semi-Urban Recovery – Field-First with Digital Enablement

Context

A microfinance institution operating in semi-urban regions traditionally relied on field agents for collections. To improve efficiency and reduce delays, the organization introduced digital tools alongside its field-first approach.

Approach

1. **Digital Empowerment of Field Agents**

   - **Mobile Apps for Agents:** Field agents were equipped with mobile applications to log interactions, update repayment statuses, and generate digital receipts instantly.

   - **Data Synchronization:** Real-time syncing of repayment data ensured that management had up-to-date information on collections progress.

2. **Borrower Digital Onboarding**

   - **Promoting Digital Payments:** During field visits, agents educated borrowers about digital payment channels, such as UPI and mobile wallets, and assisted them in setting up accounts.

   - **Automated SMS Reminders:** Borrowers received SMS reminders for upcoming payments, encouraging timely repayment and reducing manual follow-ups.

Outcome

- **Improved Repayment Rates:** The hybrid approach led to a 25% increase in repayment rates by addressing delays and improving operational tracking.

- **Enhanced Digital Adoption:** A 40% increase in borrowers using digital payment channels was achieved, reducing long-term dependency on field agents.

- **Operational Efficiency:** Field agents' productivity improved as digital tools streamlined their workflows, allowing them to handle more cases effectively.

Key Insights from Case Studies

1. **Urban vs. Semi-Urban Strategies:**

   - Urban areas benefit more from digital-first approaches, with field support reserved for escalated cases.

   - Semi-urban regions require a field-first approach initially, but digital enablement gradually reduces reliance on manual processes.

2. **Hybrid Models Enhance Efficiency:**

   - Combining digital and field strategies optimizes resource allocation and recovery rates.

   - Digital tools complement field efforts, improving tracking, reporting, and borrower engagement.

3. **Adaptability is Key:**

   - Tailoring the hybrid model to borrower demographics and geographic challenges ensures higher success rates.

By integrating field collections with digital tools, financial institutions can achieve scalable, cost-efficient, and borrower-friendly recovery models adaptable to various contexts.

Conclusion: Striking the Right Balance

The landscape of collections has transformed significantly with the advent of digital tools and analytics-driven strategies. Yet, this evolution underscores a critical realization: no single approach is universally effective. The interplay between digital and field collections offers financial institutions a balanced, flexible framework for navigating the complexities of recovery processes.

The Power of Digital-First Strategies

Digital-first collections have revolutionized how institutions interact with borrowers, offering:

1. **Scalability:** Automated systems enable organizations to manage thousands of accounts simultaneously, ensuring timely outreach without the limitations of human capacity.

2. **Cost-Effectiveness:** By reducing dependency on field agents and manual processes, digital approaches significantly cut operational expenses.

3. **Enhanced Borrower Convenience:** 24/7 accessibility, self-service options, and personalized nudges provide a borrower-centric experience, fostering better engagement and repayment behaviour.

4. **Data-Driven Precision:** Advanced analytics allow institutions to identify high-risk accounts, predict delinquencies, and design tailored strategies to maximize recovery.

5. **Compliance and Transparency:** Automated tools ensure adherence to regulatory requirements, reducing

the risk of legal challenges and providing an auditable trail of borrower interactions.

Despite these advantages, the digital-first model is not without its limitations. The digital divide, resistance to automated engagement, and the inability to address complex, emotionally sensitive cases mean that field collections remain indispensable.

The Undeniable Role of Field Collections

Field collections bring an irreplaceable human touch to scenarios where personal interaction is crucial:

1. **Addressing High-Value and Sensitive Cases:** Personal visits foster trust and demonstrate the institution's commitment to resolving disputes amicably.

2. **Resolving Complex Issues:** Face-to-face engagement facilitates detailed discussions and quicker resolution of disputes involving documentation errors or contested balances.

3. **Empathy in Financial Distress:** Borrowers facing hardships, such as job losses or medical emergencies, often respond better to empathetic in-person support.

4. **Overcoming Low-Digital Penetration:** In rural and semi-urban areas, where digital adoption is limited, field agents ensure consistent communication and effective recovery.

However, field collections are resource-intensive and less scalable, making it essential to integrate them thoughtfully into the broader strategy.

The Promise of Hybrid Models

Hybrid models combine the strengths of both approaches, enabling institutions to create a resilient and adaptive recovery framework.

1. **Optimizing Resource Allocation:**

   - Digital tools handle routine tasks like reminders and follow-ups, allowing field agents to focus on escalated or high-value cases.

   - Resources are allocated based on risk profiles and borrower behaviour, maximizing efficiency.

2. **Enhancing Customer Experience:**

   - Borrowers benefit from the convenience of digital channels while retaining the option for personal interaction when necessary.

   - Hybrid approaches maintain a balance between automation and human touch, fostering trust and satisfaction.

3. **Improving Recovery Outcomes:**

   - Data from digital channels informs field strategies, enabling agents to approach borrowers with insights that increase the likelihood of resolution.

   - Institutions can achieve higher recovery rates by addressing both the scale of digital-first strategies and the depth of field engagement.

Building the Future of Collections

Financial institutions must adopt a forward-looking perspective to succeed in an increasingly dynamic environment:

1. **Investment in Technology:**

   - Advanced analytics, AI, and automation must continue to underpin digital strategies, driving predictive capabilities and operational efficiency.

2. **Field Empowerment:**

   - Equip field agents with digital tools for real-time data access, efficient task management, and transparent borrower interactions.

3. **Customer-Centric Design:**

   - Both digital and field strategies must prioritize borrower convenience and empathy, ensuring that the collections process supports long-term relationships.

4. **Agile Governance Models:**

   - Cross-functional collaboration between collections, legal, customer service, and other teams ensures cohesive execution of hybrid strategies.

Final Thoughts

The evolution of collections strategies underscores the complementary nature of digital and field approaches. Digital-first strategies offer unparalleled scalability, efficiency, and data-driven precision, while field collections bring empathy, trust, and resolution to the most complex scenarios. Hybrid models, blending these strengths, represent the pinnacle of modern recovery frameworks.

By embracing a balanced approach, financial institutions can not only optimize recovery rates but also enhance borrower relationships and operational efficiency. This balance is not just a strategy for effective collections—it is a roadmap for sustainable, customer-centric growth in an ever-changing financial ecosystem.

"What gets measured gets managed."

— Peter Drucker

- **Attributed to:** Peter F. Drucker, widely regarded as the father of modern management.

- **Background:** This principle applies universally in management, including collections, highlighting the importance of monitoring key metrics to drive performance and decision-making.

18

Metrics That Matter: Collections KPIs

18.1 Defining KPIs for Successful Collections

Key Performance Indicators (KPIs) are essential for evaluating and optimizing the effectiveness of collections strategies. In the context of collections, KPIs serve as measurable metrics that guide decision-making and drive performance across all stages of delinquency. Defining the right KPIs ensures that financial institutions can track their recovery efforts, align them with business goals, and make data-driven decisions.

KPIs in collections typically cover various dimensions, including operational efficiency, customer engagement, and financial outcomes. For example, early-stage KPIs like the **Number of Customers Visited** and **Visit Percentage** focus on proactive outreach efforts, ensuring that field agents engage with customers effectively. Mid-stage KPIs, such as **Maturity Efficiency %** and **Collections Efficiency %**, track the ability to collect payments and manage overdue obligations effectively. In late-stage delinquency, more targeted KPIs like **Resolution %**, **Reversal %**, and **Repossession** measure how well the collections team resolves long-term overdue accounts and recovers assets.

Furthermore, KPIs should be aligned with delinquency buckets and target rates. By measuring metrics such as **Collection %**, **Collection Amount**, and **Settlement Termination**, institutions can assess the success of their collections strategies in minimizing losses and improving recovery rates. Defining these KPIs allows institutions to set clear goals, monitor performance, and implement corrective actions, when necessary, ultimately driving successful collections and better financial outcomes.

18.2   Importance of KPIs in Collections

Key Performance Indicators (KPIs) are critical for aligning collections efforts with business objectives, optimizing resource allocation, and ensuring accountability. By defining measurable outcomes, financial institutions can track progress and make data-driven decisions to improve portfolio health and recovery rates.

18.3   Core KPIs by Segment

18.3.1   Early Delinquency (1–30 DPD)

The 1–30 Days Past Due (DPD) period is a critical stage in the collections process, as it represents the initial signs of delinquency. Early delinquency KPIs play a pivotal role in mitigating risk, reducing the impact of overdue accounts, and setting the tone for recovery efforts. By focusing on proactive strategies, financial institutions can minimize the chances of accounts progressing to more severe stages of delinquency. The following KPIs are integral to tracking the effectiveness of early-stage collections:

1. **Delinquency Rate:** This KPI measures the percentage of accounts that enter the 1–30 DPD bucket. It serves as an early indicator of delinquency trends, helping organizations monitor the influx of overdue accounts and assess the overall health of their portfolio. A rising delinquency rate can signal the need for corrective action in credit risk assessment, underwriting practices, or the implementation of early intervention strategies.

2. **Right Party Contact (RPC) Rate:** The RPC Rate measures the success of the collections team in contacting the correct borrower. This KPI is vital because effective communication is the foundation of resolving delinquencies. A high RPC rate indicates that the collections team is reaching the right individuals, which increases the likelihood of engagement and repayment discussions. Low RPC rates may indicate issues with contact information or ineffective outreach strategies.

3. **Promise-to-Pay (PTP) Conversion Rate:** This metric tracks the percentage of borrowers who commit to a repayment plan (Promise-to-Pay) after initial contact. The PTP Conversion Rate is a key indicator of how well the collections team can negotiate and encourage borrowers to agree to structured repayment terms. A high conversion rate suggests that borrowers are willing to cooperate, which can result in a quicker recovery of overdue balances.

4. **First Contact Resolution Rate (FCR):** The FCR Rate measures the percentage of accounts that are resolved during the first interaction with the borrower. This KPI

is critical for gauging the efficiency of the collections process. A high FCR rate means that the collections team is effectively addressing the issues and finding solutions on the first call or visit, thereby reducing the need for repeated follow-ups and improving overall operational efficiency. Low FCR rates may indicate the need for further training or system improvements in handling early-stage delinquencies.

5. **Recovery Rate:** The Recovery Rate measures the amount recovered as a percentage of the total overdue balance in the 1–30 DPD bucket. It reflects the effectiveness of collections efforts in recouping funds early in the delinquency cycle. A high recovery rate indicates that the institution can recover significant amounts before accounts become severely delinquent, reducing the overall risk of bad debts. Monitoring this rate helps identify whether collections teams are engaging borrowers effectively and recovering funds efficiently at the early stages.

Together, these KPIs provide a comprehensive overview of the early delinquency phase. By continuously monitoring these indicators, financial institutions can make data-driven decisions, optimize their collections strategies, and ultimately reduce the likelihood of accounts progressing to more serious delinquency buckets.

18.3.2 Mid-Stage Delinquency (30–90 DPD)

The 30–90 Days Past Due (DPD) stage represents the middle phase of delinquency and often requires more aggressive intervention strategies compared to early delinquency.

Accounts in this stage are at a higher risk of progressing to severe delinquency (90+ DPD or charge-off), making it essential for financial institutions to closely monitor and manage collections efforts. The following KPIs are key to evaluating performance in this stage:

1. **Roll-Back Rate:** The Roll-Back Rate measures the percentage of accounts that revert from the 30–90 DPD bucket back to the current (1–30 DPD) status. This KPI is an indicator of the effectiveness of collections teams in resolving delinquencies before they escalate further. A high roll-back rate suggests that collections efforts, such as early intervention and restructuring payment plans, are successful in re-establishing regular payment behaviours. A low roll-back rate could indicate that additional measures or different strategies are required to prevent accounts from worsening.

2. **Skip Tracing Effectiveness:** Skip tracing is a crucial tool for locating and re-establishing contact with borrowers who have become unresponsive or difficult to reach. This KPI measures the success rate of collections teams in identifying and contacting these individuals. As borrowers move, change phone numbers, or otherwise attempt to avoid communication, effective skip tracing strategies—such as using alternative contact information, public records, or third-party data providers—become essential. High skip tracing effectiveness ensures that collections teams can continue to engage borrowers and resolve delinquencies, reducing the risk of default or further delinquency.

3. **Agent Productivity Metrics:** Productivity metrics play an important role in evaluating the efficiency of collections agents handling mid-stage delinquencies. Key productivity metrics include:

   o **Accounts Handled per Agent**: This metric measures the number of accounts that each agent is responsible for during a specific period. It serves as an indicator of workload distribution and efficiency. A higher number of accounts handled per agent can suggest effective use of resources, but if the volume is too high, it could lead to burnout or decreased performance. Tracking this metric helps organizations balance agent workload and optimize staffing levels.

   o **Amount Recovered per Agent**: This metric tracks the total amount of overdue funds recovered by each agent. It directly reflects the agent's effectiveness in recovering outstanding balances during the mid-stage delinquency phase. A high recovery per agent suggests that agents are focused on resolving delinquencies efficiently, while a lower figure may indicate that further training or support is needed to improve recovery outcomes.

4. **Resolution Time:** The Resolution Time measures the average time taken to resolve cases within the 30–90 DPD bucket. This KPI is critical for assessing how quickly and efficiently collections agents can address and resolve delinquencies before accounts move into

the 90+ DPD stage. A shorter resolution time indicates that the collections team is effective in engaging borrowers, negotiating payment plans, or taking other necessary actions to clear delinquencies. Longer resolution times can signal inefficiencies or delays in the collections process, requiring analysis to identify areas for improvement, such as process bottlenecks or inadequate agent training.

By monitoring these KPIs in the 30–90 DPD stage, financial institutions can identify trends, make informed decisions about resource allocation, and adjust their collections strategies to reduce the risk of further escalation. Mid-stage delinquencies are critical to manage effectively, as this is where financial institutions can have the greatest impact in preventing more severe delinquencies and maintaining the overall health of the loan portfolio.

18.2.3   Late-Stage Delinquency (90+ DPD)

The 90+ Days Past Due (DPD) stage represents the critical point of delinquency where accounts have significantly worsened, and the likelihood of full recovery without strong intervention is reduced. At this stage, collections efforts require a more strategic and often aggressive approach, as customers are at the brink of default, and the risks to the financial institution's portfolio are higher. The following KPIs are critical for evaluating collections performance in the late-stage delinquency phase:

1. **Legal Action Conversion Rate:** The Legal Action Conversion Rate measures the percentage of accounts in

the 90+ DPD bucket that are escalated to legal action or repossession. This KPI helps assess how many delinquent accounts have reached a point where more formal and severe measures, such as initiating legal proceedings or reclaiming assets, are necessary. A higher conversion rate indicates that the collections team is effectively identifying high-risk accounts that may require legal or repossession action to recover the owed amount. However, an excessively high rate may suggest that earlier interventions were insufficient, or that accounts are not being resolved before they escalate to this point. This metric is important for understanding the shift in collections tactics from soft collection strategies to more intensive recovery measures.

2. **Write-Off Recovery Rate:** The Write-Off Recovery Rate measures the amount recovered from accounts that were previously written off as bad debt, expressed as a percentage of the total written-off portfolio. Financial institutions often write off certain accounts after they have remained delinquent for an extended period, but recovery efforts can continue. This KPI indicates how successful the institution is in recovering funds from these written-off accounts through ongoing collections, settlements, or other means. A higher write-off recovery rate suggests that there are opportunities to recover funds even from accounts that were deemed uncollectible, which directly impacts the bottom line and improves the financial institution's overall recovery performance.

3. **Average Cost per Recovery:** The Average Cost per Recovery tracks the operational cost incurred for each successful recovery in the late-stage delinquency bucket. This KPI is essential for understanding the cost-efficiency of the collections process during the most intensive phase of recovery. Costs may include legal fees, collection agency commissions, field agent visits, and administrative costs associated with handling legal or repossession cases. While collections efforts at this stage may be more expensive due to the complexity of the cases, a lower average cost per recovery indicates that the process is efficient and that resources are being utilized effectively. On the other hand, a high cost per recovery could signal inefficiencies or areas where cost control measures need to be implemented.

4. **Settlement Rate:** The Settlement Rate measures the percentage of late-stage delinquent accounts that are resolved through settlements or restructuring agreements. Settlements or restructuring options allow borrowers to agree on a modified repayment plan or a reduced lump sum payment to settle their outstanding debt. This KPI reflects how effective the collections team is in negotiating favourable outcomes for both the institution and the borrower. A higher settlement rate suggests that borrowers are more willing to cooperate with modified terms, or that the collections team is skilled at facilitating mutually beneficial resolutions. A lower settlement rate could indicate resistance from borrowers to accept new terms, or that the institution

is not offering attractive settlement options. It's important for the collections team to evaluate this KPI in conjunction with other factors, such as recovery rates, to ensure that settlements are being offered where they are likely to provide the best recovery outcome.

Significance of These KPIs:

In the late-stage delinquency phase, financial institutions are dealing with high-risk, hard-to-collect accounts. These KPIs help institutions track the effectiveness of their aggressive recovery measures and ensure that they are making the best possible decisions regarding escalation, legal action, or settlements. By monitoring the **Legal Action Conversion Rate**, institutions can assess whether legal action is being appropriately utilized and whether the right accounts are being pursued through formal recovery methods. Similarly, tracking **Write-Off Recovery Rate** highlights opportunities to recapture losses from accounts that have been written off, improving the overall financial health of the institution.

The **Average Cost per Recovery** serves as a critical gauge for balancing recovery success with operational efficiency, ensuring that resources are being used cost-effectively. Finally, the **Settlement Rate** provides valuable insights into how well the institution is managing disputes and negotiating with borrowers to reach amicable resolutions. Overall, the management of late-stage delinquencies requires a delicate balance of aggressive recovery tactics, operational cost control, and maintaining a willingness to negotiate terms that will result in the best possible recovery outcomes for both the borrower and the institution.

18.4   The Science of Tracking and Measuring Productivity

18.4.1   Productivity Metrics

Tracking individual and team productivity in collections is critical for optimizing resource allocation and ensuring that efforts are aligned with organizational goals. Productivity metrics provide insights into the effectiveness and efficiency of agents, allowing management to identify strengths, areas for improvement, and potential bottlenecks. These metrics also ensure that agents are working efficiently within the framework of the institution's recovery strategy while maintaining a high level of service and compliance with regulatory standards. Below are the key productivity metrics that can help gauge the performance of collections teams effectively:

Key Metrics:

1. **Accounts Handled per Agent**: This metric tracks the number of delinquent accounts assigned to an agent over a defined period (daily, weekly, or monthly). The **Accounts Handled per Agent** metric helps in assessing the workload distribution and overall capacity of each agent. By analysing this data, managers can identify if agents are being overloaded, which could negatively affect performance and recovery outcomes, or underutilized, potentially leading to inefficiencies.

Ideally, a balanced distribution of accounts ensures that agents have a manageable caseload, allowing them to focus on high-priority cases while maintaining overall productivity.

A high number of accounts handled can be an indicator of efficiency, but it is essential to ensure that this does not compromise the quality of engagement with each customer. For optimal performance, this metric should be used in conjunction with other quality indicators, such as **Resolution Rate per Agent** and **Contact Success Rate**, to ensure agents can manage the accounts without sacrificing their ability to resolve cases effectively.

2. **Resolution Rate per Agent**: The **Resolution Rate per Agent** measures the percentage of delinquent accounts that an agent successfully resolves within a set timeframe (e.g., daily, weekly, or monthly). Resolution could be defined as full repayment, restructured payments, settlements, or normalization of the account status. This metric is critical for evaluating the effectiveness of agents in bringing accounts to resolution and recovering outstanding balances.

A higher resolution rate is indicative of an agent's ability to handle cases efficiently and effectively, demonstrating strong negotiation skills, product knowledge, and communication abilities. It also helps track the agent's ability to convert delinquent accounts into active accounts through direct resolution or payment arrangements. If the resolution rate is low, it may indicate that agents require additional training or that certain processes need to be improved to facilitate quicker resolutions.

3. **Recovery Efficiency**: **Recovery Efficiency** measures the amount recovered per hour worked or per case handled. This metric is designed to evaluate the economic performance of the collections process, highlighting how effectively agents are turning delinquent accounts into recovered funds. Recovery efficiency can be calculated by dividing the total amount recovered by the total number of hours worked or the total number of cases handled by an agent or team.

   This metric provides a valuable indication of the effectiveness of collections efforts in terms of return on time or effort invested. It helps to assess the productivity of the collections team in real terms, ensuring that agents are not only managing a high number of accounts but are also maximizing the amount recovered from those accounts. A high recovery efficiency implies that the agents can resolve cases quickly and efficiently while recovering a significant portion of the overdue balances.

4. **Contact Success Rate**: The **Contact Success Rate** measures the ratio of successful borrower contacts to the total number of outreach attempts made by an agent. A successful contact typically refers to making meaningful communication with the borrower, which may result in a payment arrangement, promise-to-pay (PTP), or agreement to engage in further negotiations.

This metric is crucial for understanding how effectively an agent is connecting with borrowers and overcoming barriers to contact, such as disconnected phone lines, wrong numbers, or unresponsive customers.

A high **Contact Success Rate** indicates that the agent is skilled at reaching borrowers, which is crucial for progressing toward resolving delinquent accounts. If the rate is low, it could point to issues with the contact strategy or the quality of contact information, requiring adjustments in outreach methods, or leveraging alternative communication channels like email, SMS, or digital platforms (e.g., WhatsApp, mobile apps). This metric can also highlight training needs for agents in terms of call techniques or customer engagement.

5. **Agent CSAT (Customer Satisfaction) Scores**: **Agent CSAT Scores** track customer satisfaction levels based on their interactions with a specific collections agent. These scores are typically gathered through post-interaction surveys or feedback mechanisms and are a direct reflection of the customer's experience during the collections process. A high CSAT score indicates that the agent handled the interaction in a professional, empathetic, and effective manner, which can help to preserve customer relationships even when dealing with financial difficulties.

Measuring CSAT is essential because it aligns with the institution's goal of balancing recovery with customer service. While collections efforts are focused on recovering overdue amounts, maintaining a positive borrower experience is equally important for customer retention, brand reputation, and minimizing disputes or complaints. Monitoring agent CSAT scores enables management to ensure that collections agents are adhering to service standards and demonstrating the empathy and professionalism required to resolve issues without escalating customer frustration.

CSAT Scores are often used alongside other qualitative metrics, such as complaints or disputes raised by customers, to assess the overall impact of collections strategies on customer experience.

Significance of Productivity Metrics:

Together, these productivity metrics help managers and collections teams understand both the quantity and quality of their efforts. While individual productivity is important for day-to-day operations, it is equally crucial to monitor the effectiveness of those efforts in terms of actual recovery and customer satisfaction. These metrics provide a comprehensive view of agent performance, pinpointing areas for improvement in terms of time management, customer engagement, and financial recovery.

By regularly tracking and analysing **Accounts Handled per Agent**, **Resolution Rate per Agent**, **Recovery Efficiency**, **Contact Success Rate**, and **Agent CSAT Scores**, financial institutions can better allocate resources, optimize agent performance, and ultimately improve recovery rates across different stages of delinquency. This data-driven approach not only enhances operational efficiency but also ensures that the institution's collections process remains customer-centric and focused on long-term, sustainable success.

18.4.2   Tools for Productivity Measurement

- **CRM Platforms**: Provide real-time data on agent performance, task completion, and borrower interactions.

- **Workforce Management Systems**: Allocate tasks based on agent expertise and monitor their execution.

- **Predictive Analytics Tools**: Help prioritize high-risk accounts, improving agent focus and efficiency.

18.4.3   Benchmarking Productivity

- Establish KPIs based on portfolio size, customer segment, and geographical reach.

- Use industry standards to benchmark performance and identify areas for improvement.

18.5   Performance Dashboards

Organizational-Level KPIs

Category	KPI	Description	Frequency
Portfolio Health	Delinquency Rate (DR)	Percentage of accounts that are past due.	Daily/ Weekly
	Portfolio at Risk (PAR)	Value of loans in delinquency buckets as a % of total portfolio.	Weekly/ Monthly
	Write-Off Rate	Percentage of loans written off as unrecoverable.	Monthly
Recovery Metrics	Collection Efficiency (%)	Collections as % of total demand for a specific period.	Daily/ Weekly
	Recovery Rate (%)	Recovery amount as % of total delinquency.	Monthly
Trends	Roll Forward/ Backward Rates	Movement of cases between delinquency buckets.	Weekly/ Monthly
	Attrition in Delinquent Cases	Percentage of accounts that exited delinquency buckets.	Monthly
Digital Metrics	Digital Collections Ratio	Share of total collections achieved digitally.	Weekly/ Monthly
	Self-Cure Rate	Percentage of accounts that self-pay without intervention.	Weekly/ Monthly
	Customer Engagement Index	Composite metric tracking contact, response, and promise-to-pay adherence rates.	Monthly

Category	KPI	Description	Frequency
Regulatory Metrics	Regulatory Compliance Score	Adherence to legal and regulatory standards in collections.	Monthly
Field Metrics	Distance Efficiency (%)	Collections achieved per km travelled by field executives.	Weekly
	Field Success Rate	Ratio of successful field visits to total field visits.	Weekly/ Monthly

Managerial-Level KPIs

Category	KPI	Description	Frequency
Productivity	Visits per Day per Executive	Number of customer visits conducted daily.	Daily/Weekly
	Amount Collected per Visit	Average amount collected during each customer visit.	Weekly
Portfolio Analysis	Coverage Ratio (CR)	% of allocated accounts that were contacted or visited.	Weekly
	Aging Analysis	Breakdown of cases based on aging (30, 60, 90+ DPD).	Weekly
	Bucket Flow Efficiency (%)	% of cases successfully resolved within a bucket.	Weekly/ Monthly
Team Metrics	Team Utilization Rate (%)	Actual time spent on productive activities vs. available time.	Weekly
	Supervisor Call Audit Score	Quality of supervisor follow-ups with customers and field teams.	Weekly

Category	KPI	Description	Frequency
	Dispositions Validity (%)	% of dispositions validated against geo and time compliance.	Real-time/ Weekly
Compliance Metrics	Geo-Tagging Accuracy (%)	Dispositions logged with valid geo-tagging within acceptable radius.	Real-time
Cost Metrics	Cost of Collection (COC)	Expenses incurred per dollar collected.	Monthly

Agent-Level KPIs

Category	KPI	Description	Frequency
Daily Targets	Collection Target vs. Achieved	Progress against daily, weekly, and monthly targets.	Daily
	Recovery Rate by Agent	Amount recovered vs. total allocated per agent.	Weekly
Customer Contact	Customer Contact Rate (%)	% of customers successfully contacted.	Daily/ Weekly
	Promise-to-Pay (PTP) Conversion Rate	% of PTPs honoured by customers.	Weekly
Visit Efficiency	Unique Visits per Day	Number of unique customers visited daily.	Daily
	Travel Efficiency (Distance per Visit)	Average km travelled per successful collection visit.	Weekly

Category	KPI	Description	Frequency
Compliance	Disposition Compliance (%)	% of valid dispositions logged per day.	Daily/ Weekly
	Attendance Compliance (%)	% adherence to assigned route plans and schedules.	Daily/Real-time
Performance	Revenue per Agent	Total collections per agent for a specified period.	Weekly/ Monthly

Cross-Functional KPIs (Applicable Across Levels)

Category	KPI	Description	Frequency
Customer Metrics	Customer Retention Rate (%)	Percentage of delinquent customers who return to regular repayment.	Monthly
	Net Promoter Score (NPS)	Customer satisfaction score related to collections interactions.	Monthly/ Quarterly
Predictive Insights	Probability of Default	Predictive scoring for customers at risk of default.	Weekly/ Monthly
	Collector Success Probability	Predicted success rates based on past collector performance.	Monthly

Notes:

1. **Visualization Options**:

   - Use heatmaps for geo-tagged data and coverage ratios.

   - Progress bars for daily agent targets make tracking visually intuitive.

   - Leaderboards help compare performance within teams.

2. **Real-Time Insights**:

   - Organizational and agent-level metrics like geo-compliance and collection trends should update in real time.

   - Managerial dashboards can be weekly to allow supervisors to analyse patterns.

3. **Drill-Down Features**: Each metric should allow users to explore details by filtering products, regions, or delinquency buckets.

This structured approach ensures every level of the organization has actionable insights tailored to their responsibilities.

19

Regulatory Compliance in Collections

Regulatory compliance is the cornerstone of ethical and sustainable collections practices. In an era where financial institutions are under heightened scrutiny, adhering to local and global regulations has become non-negotiable. For the collections function, this entails striking a delicate balance between recovering overdue amounts and respecting borrower rights, privacy, and dignity. Non-compliance not only results in legal penalties and reputational damage but also undermines trust with regulators, customers, and stakeholders.

This chapter explores the regulatory frameworks governing collections in the Indian and global contexts, highlighting best practices for building compliance-driven processes. From adhering to RBI guidelines to understanding global trends like data privacy and ethical collections, the focus is on creating audit-ready operations that align with modern regulatory expectations. By leveraging technology and fostering a culture of transparency, financial institutions can not only meet compliance standards but also enhance operational efficiency and customer experience.

19.1 Navigating Collections in the Indian Context: RBI Guidelines

India's regulatory framework for collections, spearheaded by the Reserve Bank of India (RBI), emphasizes fair practices, borrower rights, and ethical recovery. Institutions must understand these guidelines deeply and align their collections strategies accordingly.

Key Components of RBI Directions on Collections

1. **Fair Practices Code (FPC)**

   - **Circular Reference:** RBI Notification DBOD.Leg.No.BC.65/09.07.005/2006-07, May 2007.

   - All banks are required to adopt and implement a Fair Practices Code for their lending operations, including collections.

   - It mandates:

     - **Transparency in Communication:** Clear terms regarding repayment obligations.

     - **Fair Recovery Practices:** Collections processes must avoid harassment, intimidation, or coercion.

     - **Respecting Borrower Dignity:** Personal visits for recovery should not violate borrower privacy or dignity.

2. **Guidelines on Outsourcing of Financial Services**

   - **Circular Reference:** RBI Notification DBOD.No.BP.40/21.04.158/2006-07, November 2006.

   - Banks engaging third-party agencies for recovery must ensure:

     - Adequate due diligence and onboarding of collection agents.

     - Regular training of outsourced agents on compliance and borrower rights.

     - A grievance mechanism to address complaints related to recovery practices.

3. **Recovery Agents: Code of Conduct**

   - **Circular Reference:** RBI Circular

     DBOD.No.Leg.BC.75/09.07.005/2007-08, April 2008.

   - Banks must ensure recovery agents comply with:

     - **Time-Bound Contact Rules:** Avoiding calls or visits at unreasonable hours.

     - **Behavioural Guidelines:** Agents should act politely and without aggressive behaviour.

     - **Notification of Borrower Rights:** Informing borrowers about the actions being taken and ensuring due process.

4. **Grievance Redressal Mechanism**

   - **Circular Reference:** RBI Circular

     CEPD.PRD.No.S873/13.01.013/2021-22, Jan 2022.

   - Banks must set up a robust grievance redressal mechanism to handle borrower complaints related to collections:

     - Provide borrowers with contact details of relevant officials.

     - Escalate unresolved complaints to the RBI's Ombudsman Scheme if needed.

5. **Securitization and Reconstruction of Financial Assets and Enforcement of Security Interest Act (SARFAESI Act)**

   - **Master Direction Reference:** RBI Master Direction - RBI/DOR/2021-22/86, September 2021.

   - This framework enables banks to recover dues from secured loans through asset repossession:

     - Follow due legal process before repossession.

     - Notify borrowers adequately about defaults and impending actions.

6. **Asset Classification and Provisioning Norms**

   - **Circular Reference:** RBI Master Circular - Prudential Norms on Income Recognition, Asset Classification, and Provisioning (IRACP), July 2015.

   - Banks must classify delinquent accounts correctly into Non-Performing Assets (NPAs) and act in compliance with norms to recover dues:

     - Provide a timeline for recovery efforts before asset classification changes.

     - Ensure collections efforts align with the IRACP framework to maintain compliance.

Special Provisions for Digital Lending and Collections

- **Circular Reference:** RBI Digital Lending Guidelines – RBI/2022-23/45, August 2022.

- Digital platforms must:

  - Provide borrowers with complete loan terms upfront, including recovery processes.

  - Prohibit unauthorized access to borrower data during collections.

  - Ensure that recovery agents act within the boundaries of borrower rights, as specified by RBI.

Enforcement and Monitoring by RBI

1. **Borrower Protection**

   - Borrowers subjected to harassment can escalate their complaints directly to RBI through its Ombudsman Scheme.

   - Recovery agents found violating guidelines can lead to penalties or restrictions on the bank.

2. **Audit and Compliance**

   - Banks are required to periodically review their recovery practices and submit compliance reports to RBI.

   - Non-adherence to RBI directions can result in fines, regulatory action, or reputational risks for the institution.

Strategies for Effective Compliance in India:

1. **Agent Training Programs**:

   - Regular workshops and refresher courses on RBI guidelines and ethical practices.

   - Role-playing sessions to simulate borrower-agent interactions and refine approaches.

2. **Technology Integration**:

   - Tools like call tracking, voice recording, and compliance monitoring can ensure adherence.

   - Automated alerts for contacting borrowers outside permissible hours can prevent violations.

3. **Compliance Audits**:

   - Quarterly reviews of collection practices to identify and correct deviations.

   - Surprise audits to ensure on-ground agents follow guidelines.

4. **Borrower Communication Policies**:

   - Use standardized scripts and templates for borrower interactions to avoid ambiguity.

   - Introduce multi-lingual communication support to address regional language barriers.

Global Perspectives on Collections Compliance

Collections is a complex global challenge that transcends borders, influenced by varying cultural norms, economic conditions, and legal frameworks. Around the world, regulators have introduced distinct frameworks to ensure that collections practices remain ethical, transparent, and respectful of borrower rights. These regulations are designed to strike a balance between enabling financial institutions to recover dues and safeguarding consumers from undue harassment or exploitation.

For financial institutions operating across multiple jurisdictions, the task of maintaining compliance becomes significantly more intricate. Each country has its own set of rules governing borrower communication, data privacy, grievance redressal mechanisms, and permissible recovery methods. In addition to adhering to local laws, institutions must account for variations in enforcement practices, cultural sensitivities, and borrower expectations.

Key Global Regulations:

1. **United States (FDCPA)**:

    o   Prohibits harassment, threats, or misleading statements by collection agents.

    o   Debt information must be validated and shared with borrowers upon request.

    o   Borrowers have the right to dispute debts within a specified timeframe.

2. **European Union (GDPR)**:

   o   Borrower data must be handled securely and only for legitimate purposes.

   o   Explicit consent is required for data usage, and borrowers have the "right to be forgotten."

   o   Institutions must notify regulators and borrowers of any data breaches.

3. **United Kingdom (FCA Guidelines)**:

   o   Institutions must treat customers fairly, especially those in financial distress.

   o   Debt affordability assessments are mandatory before finalizing repayment plans.

   o   Detailed records of borrower interactions must be maintained.

Emerging Trends in Global Compliance:

1. **Data Privacy and Security**:

   o   Governments are introducing stricter laws to protect sensitive borrower information.

   o   Institutions must invest in cybersecurity and robust data management systems.

2. **Cultural Sensitivities**:

   o   Collections strategies must be adapted to regional customs and borrower expectations.

   o   Empathy is key in markets where borrowers face social stigma for loan defaults.

3. **Digitization of Compliance**:

   o   AI-driven compliance tools can identify potential breaches in real-time.

   o   Blockchain technology can enhance transparency and traceability in collections.

Best Practices for Global Compliance:

1. **Centralized Compliance Framework**:

   o   Create a unified system that incorporates region-specific regulations.

   o   Use compliance management software for consistent enforcement.

2. **Multi-Lingual Support Systems**:

   o   Enable borrowers to interact in their preferred language for better understanding and resolution.

   o   Tailor communication styles to cultural nuances.

3. **Secure Communication Channels**:

   o   Use encrypted platforms for borrower interactions to prevent data leaks.

   o   Avoid sharing sensitive information through unsecured mediums like SMS.

19.3   The Ethics of Collections

Collections can often feel adversarial—a borrower failing to repay and a lender seeking recovery. However, behind every overdue payment is a human story—unexpected medical bills, job losses, or unforeseen circumstances. The role of collections is not just to recover the money owed but to do so in a way that respects the borrower's dignity and preserves their relationship with the financial institution.

Ethics in collections is about recognizing this dual responsibility: to the institution's financial health and the customer's well-being. It's a balancing act, but when done right, it transforms collections from a transactional process into a meaningful engagement built on trust and respect.

Empathy as the Cornerstone

Imagine receiving a call about an overdue payment while already stressed about feeding your family. An empathetic collections agent can change the tone of that conversation. Instead of pressuring the borrower, they can listen, offer solutions, and create an atmosphere of support. It's not just about what is said but how it's said—tone, patience, and understanding make all the difference.

For example, if a borrower explains they've lost their job, an empathetic approach would involve discussing payment flexibility or restructuring options. This not only aids in recovery but fosters goodwill, increasing the likelihood of future business with the same customer.

Integrity in Communication

Truthful communication builds trust. Misleading a customer about penalties, deadlines, or legal consequences to pressure repayment may yield short-term results but damages long-term relationships. Borrowers deserve clarity about their obligations and rights.

For instance, if legal action is unlikely but mentioned as a threat, it erodes the customer's trust in the institution. Instead, clear guidance on next steps—whether repayment plans or consequences—empowers customers to make informed decisions.

Technology Supporting Ethical Practices

Technology can ensure ethical practices are upheld consistently. Automated reminders sent via SMS or email respect the borrower's privacy while maintaining professionalism. Advanced analytics can identify customers in financial distress, enabling personalized and humane approaches rather than blanket recovery tactics.

Handling Sensitive Cases with Care

Ethical collections shine in moments of genuine customer hardship. Suppose a customer is unable to pay due to a terminal illness in the family. Instead of escalating, the agent can work with the borrower to find a manageable solution—deferring payments, waiving penalties, or restructuring the loan.

These decisions are not only ethical but strategic; they preserve the institution's reputation and often result in eventual repayment, as the customer feels supported rather than alienated.

The Business Case for Ethics

Ethical collections are not just morally correct—they're financially sound. Customers treated with respect are more likely to repay their debts, recommend the institution to others, and return for future financial needs. Conversely, unethical practices lead to complaints, regulatory fines, and reputational damage, which can outweigh any short-term recovery gains.

Conclusion

In collections, ethics is not an optional add-on; it's the foundation of sustainable success. By prioritizing empathy, transparency, and fairness, financial institutions can recover debts while preserving the trust and loyalty of their customers. After all, collections are not just about the money—it's about the people.

19.4   Building Processes for Audit-Ready Operations

To ensure compliance sustainability, institutions must establish processes that not only adhere to regulations but also withstand scrutiny during internal and external audits.

Key Components of Audit-Ready Processes:

To ensure compliance with regulatory requirements and maintain transparency in collections, financial institutions must implement robust, audit-ready processes. These processes safeguard against violations, enhance accountability, and streamline audit preparation. Below is a detailed breakdown of the key components:

1. Documentation

Proper documentation serves as the foundation of an audit-ready process, ensuring that every interaction and decision is traceable.

- **Detailed Records of Borrower Interactions:**

  - Maintain a log of all communications with borrowers, including timestamps, method (call, email, SMS, in-person), and the content of interactions.

  - Record payment promises, grievances, and resolutions systematically to ensure traceability.

  - Keep records of legal notices, settlement agreements, and repossession documents as part of the audit trail.

- **Grievance Redressal Logs:**

  - Document all complaints raised by borrowers along with the resolution steps and timelines.

  - Ensure resolution logs include borrower satisfaction confirmation, demonstrating responsiveness and fairness.

2. Workflow Automation

Automation enhances efficiency, reduces manual errors, and ensures consistency in compliance efforts.

- **Automated Task Management:**

  - Utilize automated workflows for assigning and tracking collections tasks. For instance, flagging accounts for follow-up based on delinquency stages or payment patterns.

- Ensure tasks are logged and tracked for completion within defined timelines, reducing the scope for oversight.

- **Compliance Checks:**

  - Integrate automated compliance validation tools that:

    - Monitor agent interactions to identify potential deviations from regulatory norms.

    - Trigger alerts for cases that exceed permissible contact attempts or timing violations.

3. Real-Time Reporting

Reporting is vital for identifying trends, monitoring compliance, and responding promptly to potential issues.

- **Actionable Dashboards:**

  - Deploy dashboards that present real-time metrics such as:

    - **Grievance Resolution Rates:** The percentage of complaints resolved within regulatory timelines.

    - **Agent Adherence:** Monitoring agent behaviour against compliance guidelines like call timings and borrower interactions.

    - **Recovery Metrics:** Collection amounts and account rollbacks aligned with compliance thresholds.

3. Audit-Ready Reports:

- Generate customizable, exportable reports that align with regulatory audit requirements.

- Include compliance-related summaries such as the number of grievances handled, escalation trends, and borrower interaction logs.

4. Escalation Management

An effective escalation process ensures swift resolution of compliance breaches and maintains oversight for high-risk cases.

- **Defined Protocols:**

  - Create a structured escalation hierarchy, detailing:

    - Cases requiring immediate legal intervention (e.g., harassment complaints or data breaches).

    - Accounts flagged for severe compliance risks or borrower disputes.

- **Senior Management Oversight:**

  - Ensure escalated cases receive attention from senior managers or compliance officers.

  - Document resolutions of escalated cases to demonstrate proactive compliance management to auditors.

Building audit-ready processes is not just about meeting regulatory requirements but also about fostering a culture of transparency and accountability. By focusing on meticulous documentation, leveraging automation, enabling real-time reporting, and establishing strong escalation mechanisms, financial institutions can enhance compliance and prepare effectively for audits. These processes protect against legal risks and uphold the organization's reputation in the marketplace.

"The speed of the boss is the speed of the team."

— Lee Iacocca

- **Attributed to:** Lee Iacocca, a renowned American automobile executive who led Chrysler out of bankruptcy in the 1980s.

- **Background:** This quote emphasizes leadership's impact on team performance. In collections, it points to the importance of effective supervisors and leaders in inspiring field executives and other team members.

20

Leadership in Collections

Leadership in collections is not merely about driving recovery rates; it involves creating a balanced strategy that empowers teams, uses technology effectively, ensures compliance, and delivers customer-centric solutions. This expanded section delves into the nuances of building high-performing teams, motivating and retaining agents, and making informed decisions in complex scenarios.

20.1 Building and Leading High-Performance Collections Teams

Building a successful collections team requires more than hiring skilled professionals. It involves fostering an environment where team members are empowered, aligned, and continuously improving.

Key Elements:

1. **Skill-Based Recruitment:**

   - **Importance:** Effective collections require agents who can manage stress, communicate clearly, and adapt to diverse scenarios.

   - **Field Agents:** Prioritize local language skills, knowledge of the area, and cultural sensitivity.

- ○ **Digital Agents:** Focus on technical skills, familiarity with collection software, and analytical capabilities.

2. **Continuous Training Programs:**

- ○ **Why It Matters:** The regulatory landscape, customer expectations, and technology evolve rapidly.

- ○ **Implementation:**

  - ▪ Provide onboarding programs to familiarize new hires with organizational policies, tools, and targets.

  - ▪ Regularly update agents on new compliance requirements and customer interaction best practices.

3. **Clear Role Definition:**

- ○ Ambiguity in roles leads to inefficiencies and overlapping responsibilities.

- ○ Clearly define expectations, ensuring every team member knows their scope, deliverables, and escalation protocols.

4. **Culture of Collaboration:**

- ○ Collections teams do not work in isolation. Cross-functional collaboration with customer service, legal, and risk management improves recovery strategies and customer satisfaction.

- ○ Use integrated platforms where teams can share insights and updates in real-time.

20.2 Motivation and Retention Strategies for Field and Digital Agents

High attrition rates in collections can disrupt operations and impact recovery. Motivated agents are more productive, compliant, and engaged, ensuring better results.

Strategies to Motivate and Retain Talent:

1. **Performance-Based Incentives:**

   - **Why It Works:** Financial rewards drive short-term motivation but must be complemented by long-term growth opportunities.

   - **Implementation:**

     - Incentivize agents for recovery rates, compliance adherence, and customer satisfaction scores.

     - Avoid overemphasis on recovery, which may lead to unethical practices.

2. **Career Progression Opportunities:**

   - **Issue:** Many agents see collections as a stepping stone, not a career.

   - **Solution:**

     - Map out career pathways, offering leadership programs for high-performing agents.

     - Sponsor certifications in negotiation, analytics, or compliance.

3. **Work-Life Balance:**

   o **Challenges for Field Agents:** Long hours, extensive travel, and customer rejections lead to burnout.

   o **Strategies:**

      ▪ Provide flexible schedules, regular health checkups, and leave policies.

      ▪ Use technology to minimize manual reporting and administrative tasks.

4. **Technology Enablement:**

   o **Impact:** Simplifies workflows and boosts productivity.

   o Equip agents with mobile apps for real-time updates, route optimization, and borrower history.

5. **Team Recognition and Engagement:**

   o **Importance:** Recognition fosters loyalty and pride in work.

   o **Methods:**

      ▪ Celebrate monthly and annual achievements.

      ▪ Conduct team-building activities to strengthen camaraderie.

20.3 Decision-Making in Complex Collections Scenarios

Complex scenarios in collections often involve multiple factors, such as financial stress, regulatory risks, and customer grievances. Leadership must ensure decisions are balanced, ethical, and result-oriented.

Guiding Principles:

1. **Data-Driven Insights:**

   - **Role of Data:** Data helps prioritize high-risk accounts, predict repayment behaviours, and assess agent performance.

   - **Tools:** Use predictive analytics to allocate resources efficiently and improve decision accuracy.

2. **Balanced Judgment:**

   - Collections leaders must balance organizational goals with ethical considerations.

   - Example: For hardship cases, restructuring loans or offering settlements might be better than aggressive collections.

3. **Scenario-Based Planning:**

   - **Why It Matters:** Preparedness ensures consistency and reduces errors in handling complex cases.

   - **Approach:**

     - Create playbooks for scenarios like disputes, escalations, or legal interventions.

     - Train agents on these playbooks to ensure uniformity in execution.

4. **Crisis Management:**

   - **Challenges:** Economic downturns, regulatory audits, or sudden workload spikes demand quick and efficient responses.

   - **Leadership Role:**

     - Have contingency plans for scenarios like increased delinquency rates.

     - Use technology and temporary workforce augmentation to manage sudden demand.

Common Mistakes and Mitigation Strategies in Building Quality Teams

1. **Underestimating Training Needs:**

   - **Mistake:** Assuming agents can learn on the job.

   - **Mitigation:** Create structured, role-specific training programs with periodic refreshers.

2. **Neglecting Soft Skills:**

   - **Mistake:** Focusing solely on hard targets like recovery rates.

   - **Mitigation:** Incorporate empathy, negotiation, and communication training into development programs.

3. **Lack of Performance Feedback:**

   - **Mistake:** Agents remain unaware of areas for improvement.

   - **Mitigation:** Conduct regular one-on-one reviews, using performance metrics and customer feedback to guide discussions.

4. **Ineffective Incentive Structures:**

   - **Mistake:** Rewards tied only to recovery amounts can encourage unethical practices.

   - **Mitigation:** Link incentives to recovery, compliance, and customer satisfaction metrics.

5. **Ignoring Agent Well-Being:**

   - **Mistake:** Overburdening agents without support systems.

   - **Mitigation:** Invest in wellness programs, manageable targets, and mental health resources.

6. **Low Technology Adoption:**

   - **Mistake:** Relying on manual processes reduces efficiency and increases errors.

   - **Mitigation:** Provide agents with advanced tools for tracking, reporting, and decision-making.

By addressing these areas with a strategic approach, collections leaders can ensure not only improved recovery rates but also a motivated and high-performing team that is prepared for future challenges.

"Success is the sum of small efforts, repeated day in and day out."

— Robert Collier

- **Attributed to:** Robert Collier, an American author of self-help and motivational books.

- **Background:** This quote is often used in personal development and business contexts to emphasize the importance of consistent effort. In collections, it reminds teams that steady, focused work leads to long-term success.

21

Preparing for the Future
of Collections

As the world of banking and financial services continues to evolve, so too must the way collections are approached. The future of collections is shaped by technological advancements, shifting market dynamics, changing customer expectations, and emerging social responsibility frameworks. In this section, we will explore how financial institutions can future-proof their collections strategies to ensure they remain effective, compliant, and customer-centric in an ever-changing environment.

21.1 Future-Proofing Collections: Adapting to Changing Market Dynamics

The landscape of collections is constantly evolving, driven by technological advancements, regulatory changes, and shifts in economic conditions. Financial institutions must be agile and proactive to stay ahead of the curve and ensure their collections processes remain effective.

Key Considerations for Future-Proofing Collections:

- **Embracing Digital Transformation:** The adoption of digital tools is not optional anymore. From AI-driven predictive models to robotic process automation

(RPA), digital transformation will continue to shape the collections function. Financial institutions must invest in the right technologies that can automate routine tasks, streamline workflows, and enhance customer interactions. Automation can ensure that collections are faster, more accurate, and cost-efficient, while also minimizing human error.

- **Data-Driven Decision Making:** The future of collections will rely heavily on data analytics and insights. Predictive analytics can help identify accounts that are likely to become delinquent, allowing institutions to take preventive action before the account enters higher-risk delinquency buckets. The ability to use data to optimize allocation, tailor repayment plans, and track customer behaviour will be essential.

- **Regulatory Compliance in an Evolving Environment:** Regulations governing collections practices are constantly being updated, and financial institutions must stay compliant with these changes. Future-proofing collections means investing in compliance management systems that ensure adherence to existing and upcoming regulations, reducing the risk of penalties and legal action.

- **Omni-Channel Collections:** As customer preferences evolve, financial institutions must be able to engage with borrowers across multiple channels. Future collections strategies will require a seamless, omni-channel approach that integrates traditional methods (like phone calls) with digital channels (like mobile apps, email, and text messaging). Ensuring that collections agents can reach customers on their preferred communication channels will enhance customer experience and increase recovery rates.

- **Agile and Scalable Infrastructure:** Market dynamics are unpredictable, and collections teams need to be prepared to scale their operations up or down depending on market conditions. Financial institutions should adopt flexible, cloud-based systems that allow them to rapidly scale their collections processes and resources as required.

21.2   The Role of ESG (Environmental, Social, Governance) in Collections

Environmental, Social, and Governance (ESG) considerations are becoming increasingly important across industries, and collections is no exception. ESG-driven practices in collections focus not only on financial returns but also on how those returns are achieved in an ethical, sustainable manner.

Key ESG Considerations in Collections:

- **Environmental Impact:** As collections teams rely more on digital tools and automation, there is potential to reduce their environmental footprint. Paperless collections processes, digital customer communications, and the elimination of manual paperwork can contribute to reducing waste and energy consumption, aligning collections practices with environmental sustainability goals.

- **Social Responsibility:** The social aspect of ESG in collections refers to how financial institutions treat their customers. Ethical collections practices are critical, and institutions must ensure they maintain a respectful, fair, and transparent approach to borrower interactions. This includes offering flexible repayment plans and working with customers to find mutually beneficial solutions that help them avoid further financial distress.

- **Fair and Transparent Governance:** Governance involves establishing clear, fair, and transparent collections practices that align with ethical standards. Financial institutions should develop policies and practices that prioritize customer rights, ensure equitable treatment across borrower segments, and mitigate the risk of legal challenges. A strong governance framework will not only reduce risks but also enhance the organization's reputation as a responsible and ethical lender.

- **ESG Reporting and Transparency:** Banks are increasingly being asked to report on their ESG performance, and this includes their collections practices. Financial institutions must be prepared to demonstrate that their collections operations align with ESG principles. This could involve tracking and reporting on the outcomes of their collections activities, such as customer satisfaction scores, resolution rates, and the sustainability of their recovery strategies.

21.3   Evolving Customer Expectations: Preparing for the New Age Borrower

The profile of the typical borrower is changing. The new age borrower is tech-savvy, increasingly values customer service, and expects more personalized, flexible options. Financial institutions need to be prepared to meet these evolving expectations and ensure that their collections strategies are aligned with the needs of modern consumers.

Key Considerations for Adapting to the New Age Borrower:

- **Personalization of Collections:** Customers expect personalized experiences across all touchpoints, including collections. Financial institutions must move away from one-size-fits-all approaches and instead use data to tailor interactions. This could involve offering customized repayment plans based on a borrower's financial situation, providing targeted payment reminders, or even leveraging AI-powered chatbots to offer 24/7 assistance.

- **Self-Service Options:** The new age borrower values convenience and autonomy. Institutions must provide self-service options that allow customers to manage their repayments, request payment extensions, or explore settlement options at their own convenience. A robust digital platform that offers such services, integrated with collections systems, can enhance customer satisfaction and reduce manual intervention.

- **Omni-Channel Communication:** Modern borrowers prefer to communicate through various channels, whether that's via mobile apps, email, SMS, or voice. Collections teams must be prepared to interact with customers on their preferred platform. Seamless integration across digital and voice-based channels will ensure that borrowers can reach out and make payments on their terms.

- **Enhanced Customer Experience:** For today's consumers, collections is not just about recovering money—it's about ensuring a positive experience throughout the process. Financial institutions must focus on customer-friendly approaches, using empathy and effective communication to resolve issues. Providing access to financial education and offering flexible solutions for repayment can help improve relationships and encourage loyalty, even in challenging circumstances.

- **Technology Integration:** Borrowers expect collections processes to be fast, efficient, and secure. Institutions must invest in technologies like AI, machine learning, and blockchain to streamline and secure the collections process. Blockchain can provide transparent and tamper-proof records of transactions, enhancing trust and reducing disputes. Additionally, AI-driven analytics can help identify the best repayment strategies based on individual borrower profiles, leading to more efficient outcomes.

Preparing for the future of collections requires an agile, forward-thinking approach. Financial institutions must anticipate the changing market dynamics, adopt sustainable practices, and meet the evolving expectations of borrowers. By leveraging technology, embracing ESG principles, and offering personalized experiences, banks can future-proof their collections processes and enhance customer satisfaction. The successful collections strategy of tomorrow will not only be efficient and compliant but also customer-centric, transparent, and socially responsible.

"In the middle of difficulty lies opportunity."

— Albert Einstein

This proverb emphasizes that while crises are challenging, they also present opportunities for growth, innovation, and strengthening relationships. In the context of banking, it suggests that financial institutions can turn a crisis into a chance to showcase resilience, adaptability, and customer support, ultimately enhancing long-term trust and stability.

22

Case Studies and Real-World Examples

Successes and Failures in Collections

1. Case Study: Importance of Integrated Legal and Collections Systems in Banking

Hypothetical Scenario: A Misstep in Coordination Between Collections and Legal Systems

In the fast-paced world of banking and financial services, coordination between different operational systems is crucial. However, in many banks and NBFCs, the collections system often focuses solely on field collections and settlement processes, while the legal workflow operates as a standalone system. This lack of integration can lead to significant operational and reputational risks, as illustrated by the following hypothetical scenario based on real-world challenges.

The Event

A large NBFC was handling a high-value case involving a fleet operator who had defaulted on a loan, pushing the account into the Non-Performing Asset (NPA) category. To recover the dues, the organization initiated legal proceedings by filing an execution petition against the borrower. The court proceedings progressed, and the case reached a critical stage where a warrant and potential imprisonment for the defaulter were imminent.

Simultaneously, the collections team, unaware of the advanced stage of legal proceedings, was actively engaging with the borrower to recover the overdue amount. As part of their efforts, the collections team offered a One-Time Settlement (OTS) to the customer, providing a 20% waiver on the principal amount to close the case. Knowing the seriousness of the legal case and the impending judgment against him, the borrower quickly accepted the OTS offer and paid the settlement amount.

The Oversight

While the settlement was processed, the legal team was not informed, nor was the legal system updated about the settlement and loan closure. Within two days, at the next court hearing, the borrower presented the court with a No Objection Certificate (NOC) and a closure letter issued by the NBFC's collections team, proving that the loan had been resolved.

The court was taken aback, and the bank had to issue a formal apology for failing to synchronize its internal processes. This incident not only embarrassed the organization but also strained its relationship with the judiciary.

Key Takeaways

1. **Operational Risk:** The lack of integration between the collections and legal systems led to a major operational

oversight, highlighting the importance of unified workflows.

2. **Reputational Risk:** Such incidents can damage the institution's credibility with stakeholders, including courts and customers.

3. **Financial Loss:** The bank potentially incurred additional legal costs, along with the risk of losing future recoveries due to weakened trust in its processes.

Conclusion

This hypothetical case underscores the critical need for an integrated collections and legal system. Such integration ensures that all teams operate with a single source of truth, minimizing the risk of contradictory actions. Legal workflows embedded within the collections system or tightly integrated with it enable real-time updates, seamless communication, and synchronized actions. This approach is not just about operational efficiency; it is about safeguarding the institution's reputation, mitigating risks, and ensuring fair and transparent treatment of customers.

2. Case Study: Streamlining Credit Shield Insurance Claims Through Automation

Real-World Scenario: Bridging Gaps in Credit Shield Claim Processing

In my previous role as Head of Collections Strategy and Centre of Excellence (CoE), I encountered a significant challenge with processing Credit Shield Insurance (CLI) claims for commercial vehicle loans. This insurance protects the borrower and their family by covering loan repayment in cases of unforeseen events such as death or disability during the loan tenure. However, a lack of awareness among customers and their families about the existence of this insurance often resulted in missed opportunities to leverage these benefits, leading to financial strain on families and higher NPAs (Non-Performing Assets) for the organization.

The Challenge

The organization maintained a pool of approximately 7 lakh customers, of which many had Credit Shield Insurance coverage. During one particular quarter, feedback captured by the collections app indicated that around 2,000 customers were reported as deceased (Customer Deceased, or CD). However, the insurance team's report showed that only 500+ CLI claims had been submitted and processed.

This disconnect between reported CD cases and processed insurance claims was alarming. It became evident that while field collection teams were identifying deceased customers, the information was not being systematically utilized to initiate and process insurance claims.

The Solution: Automated Workflow Implementation

To address this gap, I spearheaded the development of an automated workflow within the integrated Collections Management System (iCMS). The process was designed to ensure that every CD case was systematically verified, documented, and processed for an insurance claim.

Here's how the automated workflow functioned:

1. **Triggering Verification Workflow:**

   - When a field collections executive reported a CD case in the iCMS, an automated workflow would be triggered.

   - This workflow would assign the case to the collections supervisor managing that team, prompting them to contact the deceased customer's family.

2. **Verification and Documentation:**

   - The supervisor would validate the report, collect necessary documents (e.g., death certificate), and upload them into the system.

3. **Insurance Claim Initiation:**

   - Once the death certificate was uploaded, a secondary automated workflow would notify the insurance operations team.

   - The insurance team would then initiate the claim process with the insurance provider.

4. **Coordinated Communication:**

   - The workflow was further automated to handle coordination between the insurance operations team and the insurance company.

   - Queries or additional document requests from the insurance company were routed through the system to ensure prompt responses and efficient closure.

The Impact

The implementation of this automated workflow resulted in significant improvements:

- **Higher Claim Submission Rate:** All 2,000 CD cases reported were logged with the insurance company, compared to just 500+ claims previously.

- **Reduced Turnaround Time (TAT):** The automation reduced the claim processing time by 50%, as the coordination with the insurance company became seamless and real-time.

- **Financial Impact:** The streamlined process reduced NPAs by ₹10 crore within just three months, showcasing the financial benefits of automation and workflow integration.

Key Takeaways

1. **Data Synchronization:** Aligning field feedback with backend operations can uncover critical gaps and create opportunities for process improvements.

2. **Automation as a Catalyst:** Automated workflows eliminate manual errors, improve coordination, and ensure that every case is acted upon efficiently.

3. **Cross-Functional Collaboration:** Effective integration between collections, operations, and insurance teams is essential for achieving better results.

Conclusion

This experience highlighted the value of leveraging technology to bridge operational gaps. By automating the CLI claim process, the organization not only improved customer service but also achieved substantial financial and operational benefits. This case underscores the importance of proactive leadership and innovative solutions in addressing systemic challenges in collections and insurance management.

3. Case Study: Enhancing Field Executive Productivity Through Location Analytics

Real-World Scenario: Addressing Gaps in Field Visit Tracking

In my role as Head of Digital Initiatives and IT, I encountered a persistent issue with tracking and monitoring the productivity of field executives in the collections process. Initially, the organization provided handheld devices (HHDs) for field executives to log visits and collect payments. However, this system had significant limitations, particularly in verifying the authenticity of field visits and dispositions.

The Challenge

While HHDs enabled field executives to record their daily activities, there was no mechanism to track their location or verify the genuineness of their entries. As the organization transitioned to a mobile app later, which allowed for location tracking, I observed recurring anomalies in the captured data:

- **Suspicious Dispositions:** Executives frequently logged multiple dispositions from a single location within a short timeframe, often from places like their homes or nearby tea shops.

- **Misuse of Dispositions:** Many executives used dispositions to fulfil the mandatory daily visit requirement of 8 customers without genuinely visiting those locations.

- **Lack of Oversight:** Supervisors had no visibility into whether field visits were genuinely made or if travel reimbursements claimed were valid.

The Solution: Process Change and End-to-End Location Analytics

To address these issues, I spearheaded a comprehensive overhaul of the field tracking process by integrating advanced location analytics with the mobile app. The solution had three key components:

1. **Mandatory Location Verification for Dispositions:**

   - Field executives were required to punch feedback or dispositions directly from the customer's location.

   - The system automatically verified the latitude and longitude of the punch point against the customer's registered location.

   - Any discrepancies or exceptions triggered an escalation to the supervisor for review.

2. **Proximity Checks for Multiple Dispositions:**

   - If more than one disposition was logged within a 100-meter radius and did not match the customer's registered location, the system flagged these cases as potential anomalies.

- o   Escalations were raised to the supervisor to investigate and validate the entries.

3. **Automated Travel Distance Calculation:**

   - o   Google Maps integration enabled the system to calculate the actual distance travelled by field executives daily.

   - o   Travel reimbursements were automated and tied directly to verified field visits. This eliminated fraudulent claims and ensured genuine efforts were rewarded.

The Impact

The implementation of location analytics transformed field tracking and executive productivity in several ways:

- **Improved Accountability:** Field executives became more diligent in visiting customers as fake dispositions were no longer accepted.

- **Enhanced Productivity:** With supervisors actively monitoring flagged cases, the overall productivity of field executives improved by **150%**.

- **Streamlined Reimbursements:** Automated distance calculations ensured that only legitimate travel expenses were reimbursed, reducing administrative overhead and curbing misuse.

- **Data-Driven Insights:** The system provided actionable insights into field operations, enabling better route planning, resource allocation, and performance management.

Key Takeaways

1. **Technology Integration:** Leveraging mobile apps and location analytics can significantly improve field operations.

2. **Proactive Monitoring:** Setting up automated escalations for anomalies ensures accountability and transparency.

3. **Data Validation:** Tying reimbursements and performance metrics to verified data reduces fraud and enhances efficiency.

Conclusion

This initiative showcased the power of location analytics in resolving long-standing operational challenges. By aligning technology with process changes, the organization not only improved field executive accountability but also optimized operational efficiency, contributing to better collections outcomes. This experience underscores the importance of a robust monitoring framework in field-intensive operations like collections.

4. Enhancing the Effectiveness of Collection Supervision through Automated Review Mechanisms

In the traditional perception, a collections system revolves around **allocation of contracts to field executives** and a **mobile application** for those executives to facilitate collections activities. However, based on my decade-long experience in managing collections strategy, I firmly believe that these are just **10% of what a comprehensive collections system should encompass.**

The Need for an Advanced Review Mechanism

For collections to be truly effective and efficient, a **robust review mechanism** must be integrated into the automated collections journey. Supervisors play a pivotal role in ensuring adherence to strategies, maintaining productivity, and resolving escalations. However, the effectiveness of supervision largely depends on their knowledge, intent, and capability to probe into the portfolio.

Understanding Supervisor Archetypes

Supervisors in the collections ecosystem can typically be categorized into three groups based on their behaviour and approach to reviews:

1. **Category 1: The Overwhelmed Reviewer**

    o **Profile:** These supervisors have a strong intention to review but lack the knowledge or tools to do so effectively.

    o **Challenges:** They attempt to review **all field executives** and **all customer accounts** indiscriminately, leading to:

        ▪ Spending excessive time on reviews.

        ▪ Inefficient use of time and resources.

        ▪ Missing critical cases that require immediate attention due to lack of prioritization.

2. **Category 2: The Efficient Reviewer**

   - ○ **Profile:** These supervisors possess the knowledge and techniques to focus their efforts on the right customers and field executives.

   - ○ **Strengths:**

     - They identify high-priority cases and allocate their time effectively.

     - They ensure high productivity and timely escalations.

   - • **Outcome:** Their ability to probe deeply and manage time effectively leads to optimal portfolio performance.

3. **Category 3: The Nonchalant Supervisor**

   - ○ **Profile:** These supervisors lack both the intent to review and the techniques to do so.

   - ○ **Challenges:**

     - They ignore the review process, leaving the portfolio **unattended and vulnerable.**

     - Lack of oversight in this category poses a **serious threat** to the organization's collections performance.

The Solution: An Automated Review Module with Nudges

To address these challenges and ensure uniform and effective supervision across all categories of supervisors, we developed an **Automated Review Module** powered by a **rule engine** and **nudges.**

Key Features of the Review Module:

1. **Prioritized Review Recommendations:**

   - The system identifies and prioritizes customers and field executives requiring immediate attention.

   - Supervisors are nudged to:

     - **Call specific customers** and provided reasons such as missed payments, broken promises to pay, or critical DPD escalation.

     - **Visit certain customers** who are high-risk or have been unresponsive to prior contacts.

     - **Review particular field executives** based on anomalies in their performance, such as inconsistent visit patterns, low success rates, or high deviation in daily targets.

2. **Data-Driven Insights:**

   - Supervisors are presented with key metrics and justifications for each nudge, such as:

     - Customer payment behaviour trends.

     - Field executive productivity and adherence to allocation.

   - These insights eliminate guesswork and equip supervisors to make informed decisions.

3. **Dynamic Workflows:**

   - Supervisors receive real-time updates and tasks based on portfolio performance.

   - Escalations and follow-ups are automated, ensuring timely action on critical cases.

4. **Standardization Across Archetypes:**

   - By automating review recommendations, the system standardizes the approach across all supervisor categories:

     - **Category 1 supervisors** are guided to focus on the right cases, saving time and improving efficiency.

     - **Category 2 supervisors** are further empowered with advanced insights to refine their efforts.

     - **Category 3 supervisors** are nudged into action, ensuring that portfolios are not left unattended.

Benefits of the Automated Review Module:

- **Consistency in Supervision:** All supervisors operate at a higher level of efficiency, ensuring uniform performance across teams.

- **Time Optimization:** Focused reviews eliminate wasted effort on low-priority cases.

- **Improved Portfolio Health:** Proactive nudges reduce delinquency rates and improve recovery percentages.

- **Scalability:** The system can handle large portfolios seamlessly, making it ideal for organizations with diverse and geographically spread operations.

Conclusion:

The integration of an automated review module with personalized nudges revolutionizes the traditional approach to collections supervision. By leveraging technology to guide and standardize supervisory actions, banks and financial institutions can significantly enhance their collections outcomes. This system ensures that no customer or field executive is overlooked, enabling a well-coordinated and effective collections strategy.

5. Use Case: Implementing GenAI-Based Voice Bot and Chat Bot for PDM and BKT X in Collections

Overview

In my previous organization, we implemented **Generative AI-based Voice and Chat Bots** to revolutionize our collections process, specifically for **PDM (Pre-Due Management)** and **BKT X (Delinquency Management)**. The aim was to automate routine interactions, improve customer engagement, and optimize the efficiency of collections agents.

Implementation Steps

1. Understanding Business Needs and Defining Scope

- **PDM (Pre-Due Management):**

  - Send reminders to customers about upcoming EMI payments to reduce delinquency rates.

  - Answer frequently asked questions (FAQs) about payment modes, dues, and charges.

- **BKT X (Delinquency Management):**

  - Follow up with customers who missed payments, providing support for overdue cases.

  - Enable negotiations and resolution options, such as one-time settlements or EMI restructuring.

2. Technology Integration

- **Voice Bot Capabilities:**

  - AI-powered natural language understanding (NLU) for human-like conversations.

  - Real-time speech-to-text and text-to-speech functionalities for multilingual support.

  - Outbound calling to engage customers at scale.

- **Chat Bot Capabilities:**

  - Integrated with existing communication channels (e.g., WhatsApp, bank website, and mobile apps).

  - Automated responses for inquiries, status updates, and payment assistance.

- **Backend Integration:**

  - Linked with the **Integrated Collections Management System (iCMS)** for real-time updates.

  - Data integration with customer profiles, loan statuses, and payment history for personalized interactions.

3. Training the AI Models

- Trained on historical collections data, customer interaction logs, and FAQs to ensure relevance and accuracy.

- Incorporated domain-specific language and keywords used in collections.

- Regular updates for adapting to new scenarios, regulations, and customer behaviour patterns.

4. Use Cases in Action

- **For PDM:**

  - **Outbound Calls & Messages:**

    - Voice Bot calls customers 3–5 days before the due date, reminding them of upcoming payments.

    - Chat Bot sends payment reminders and links to payment portals via WhatsApp or SMS.

- **Customer Support:**

    - Handles queries about due dates, payment options, and consequences of non-payment.

    - Escalates complex queries to human agents if necessary.

- **For BKT X:**

- **Delinquency Follow-Up:**

  - Voice Bot follows up with customers 1–7 days past due, encouraging payment to avoid penalties.

  - Chat Bot provides real-time assistance for payment arrangements or negotiations.

- **Escalation Management:**

  - Identifies high-risk accounts (e.g., chronic defaulters) and routes them to specialized agents.

  - Supports automated scheduling of agent callbacks for unresolved issues.

- **Payment Facilitation:**

  - Provides UPI links, payment gateway integration, and EMI rescheduling options directly through the bot interface.

5. Feedback Loop for Continuous Improvement

- Captured feedback from customer interactions to improve accuracy and user experience.

- Analysed call and chat data to refine response scripts and enhance predictive models.

Benefits of GenAI-Based Voice and Chat Bots

1. **Operational Efficiency:**

   - Reduced dependency on human agents for routine tasks, allowing them to focus on high-value accounts.

   - Automated follow-ups and reminders reduce agent workload.

2. **Cost Savings:**

   - Handling thousands of interactions simultaneously with bots significantly lowered operational costs.

3. **Improved Customer Experience:**

   o Personalized, 24/7 support enhanced customer satisfaction.

   o Proactive communication reduced the stress of missed payments.

4. **Higher Recovery Rates:**

   o **For PDM:** Reduced delinquency rates as customers were reminded before due dates.

   o **For BKT X:** Timely follow-ups improved recovery rates by ensuring consistent engagement.

5. **Scalability:**

   o Bots could handle a large customer base across geographies without additional resources.

6. **Real-Time Insights:**

   o Generated detailed analytics on customer behaviour, enabling data-driven decisions.

Sample Outcome Metrics Post-Implementation

Metric	Before Bots	After Bots	Improve-ment
PDM Adherence Rate	70%	90%	+20%
Delinquency Follow-Up Completion	60%	95%	+35%
Cost per Interaction	₹50	₹5	-90%
Average Recovery Time (BKT X)	15 days	8 days	-47%
Customer Satisfaction Score (CSAT)	3.5/5	4.5/5	+28%

Conclusion:

Implementing a GenAI-based Voice and Chat Bot in collections proved to be a game-changer, streamlining processes, enhancing customer experience, and driving better financial outcomes. This solution not only addressed the limitations of traditional systems but also set a robust foundation for future scalability and efficiency in collections management.

<h1 style="text-align:center">23</h1>

FAQs in Collections

1. What is the best way to approach customers who are in the early stages of delinquency (1–30 DPD)?

Answer: The approach should be proactive and non-intrusive. Automated reminders through SMS, email, and phone calls are effective. The key is to offer gentle reminders without being overly aggressive. Providing clear payment options and a convenient method for repayment (like online payment links) can encourage quicker resolution.

2. How can we reduce the number of accounts that roll forward from the 30-60 DPD to 90+ DPD bucket?

Answer: Focus on early intervention and personalized follow-ups. By identifying the root causes of delinquency, such as financial hardship or temporary cash flow issues, you can offer tailored solutions like restructuring the payment terms or offering temporary relief options. Additionally, monitoring and ensuring the right allocation of accounts to experienced agents is crucial for handling cases effectively in this bucket.

3. **How do we handle accounts where customers are unresponsive or have "skipped" without leaving any trace?**

Answer: Implement skip-tracing tools and techniques. Modern collections software comes with integrated skip-tracing capabilities, including data aggregators and social media insights. Regular follow-up with automated and manual outreach methods, such as using different contact details (e.g., family members, employers), is essential to regain contact.

4. **What are the best practices for managing collections when dealing with large-scale accounts (e.g., corporate clients)?**

Answer: For large-scale or corporate clients, a customized collections strategy is essential. These clients often require a more consultative approach, with negotiations involving payment terms extensions, restructuring, or even legal action in extreme cases. Assigning specialized corporate collections teams and regularly updating risk assessments is also crucial.

5. **How can we ensure compliance with RBI guidelines and other legal frameworks during the collections process?**

Answer: Regular training and awareness programs for your collections teams are essential to ensure they are up-to-date on the latest regulations and compliance standards. Additionally, embedding compliance checks within your collections software, performing routine audits, and implementing documentation systems to track communication with customers will ensure that your process remains audit-ready.

6. How can we improve customer experience while working with delinquent accounts?

Answer: A customer-centric approach is key to improving the experience. Providing multiple, flexible payment options (such as deferred payments or instalment plans) while maintaining a respectful tone and empathetic communication can help improve customer engagement. Offering digital self-service tools and a clear grievance resolution process can also enhance the customer's perception of the collections process.

7. What is the ideal contact frequency for customers in different stages of delinquency?

Answer: The contact frequency should vary based on the delinquency stage:

- **1–30 DPD:** Weekly automated reminders, along with a phone call if necessary.

- **31–60 DPD:** Bi-weekly calls, emails, and follow-ups.

- **61–90 DPD:** Increased contact frequency, including multiple phone calls, field visits, or discussions of payment plans.

- **90+ DPD:** High-frequency contact, which may involve legal notices, field agents, and even repossession actions for secured loans.

8. How can we improve the efficiency of field collections?

Answer: To enhance field collections efficiency:

- **Route Optimization:** Use geo-location tools and route optimization software to reduce travel time and increase the number of customer visits per day.

- **Training & Performance Monitoring:** Equip field agents with advanced negotiation skills and train them on compliance and customer engagement techniques. Regularly monitor performance and provide feedback.

- **Technology Support:** Provide field agents with mobile applications to access customer information, log interactions, and provide real-time updates.

9. What role do Payment Plans play in the collections process?

Answer: Payment plans are essential for maintaining customer relationships while ensuring collections:

- **Customized Plans:** Tailor payment plans based on the borrower's financial situation. This makes it easier for them to repay the overdue balance in manageable instalments.

- **Transparency:** Clearly communicate the terms of the payment plan, including any interest or fees associated, to avoid confusion later on.

- **Automation:** Use automated systems to remind customers of upcoming payments and track adherence to the plan.

10. What are the best ways to ensure high levels of customer contact success?

Answer:

- **Multi-Channel Outreach:** Use a combination of communication channels (phone calls, emails, SMS, and even social media) to increase the likelihood of reaching the customer.

- **Personalized Communication:** Address customers by name and reference specific details about their account to make the communication more relevant.

- **Optimal Contact Time:** Research and optimize the best time to reach customers based on historical contact patterns and customer preferences.

11. How do we handle cases where customers make partial payments but don't adhere to full repayment?

Answer:

- **Follow-Up Communication:** Send timely reminders about remaining balances and discuss repayment options with the customer.

- **Escalation Strategy:** If the customer continues to avoid full repayment, escalate the issue to a senior collections agent or initiate legal proceedings if necessary.

- **Review Payment Plan:** In some cases, renegotiating the terms of the payment plan may be appropriate, but ensure there are clear consequences for non-adherence.

12. How do we manage collections for secured loans (e.g., car loans, mortgages)?

Answer:

- **Collateral Assessment:** Regularly assess the value of the collateral and ensure it covers the outstanding balance in case of default.

- **Repossession Process:** Set up clear procedures for repossession and ensure compliance with regulatory requirements for secured assets.

- **Rehabilitation Programs:** Offer customers the opportunity to reinstate the loan by catching up on overdue payments or restructuring their repayment plan.

13. What role does customer segmentation play in collections?

Answer: Customer segmentation allows for tailored collections strategies based on risk levels, account types, and payment behaviours:

- **Risk-Based Segmentation:** Identify high-risk customers early and prioritize them for more frequent follow-ups or alternative resolution strategies (e.g., settlement or restructuring).

- **Behaviour-Based Segmentation:** Use past payment behaviour to determine the most effective collections approach (e.g., early stage vs. late stage delinquency).

- **Value-Based Segmentation:** Prioritize high-value customers, ensuring that their concerns are addressed quickly to minimize portfolio impact.

14. How do we handle collections when the customer claims financial hardship?

Answer:

- **Empathetic Communication:** Acknowledge the customer's situation and offer viable solutions, such as deferring payments or restructuring terms.

- **Verification:** Request appropriate documentation to assess the genuineness of their hardship claim (e.g., loss of employment, medical emergency).

- **Offer Payment Flexibility:** In cases of genuine hardship, offer flexible repayment options such as reduced EMI or extended repayment period.

15. How can we handle customers who consistently make partial payments but do not settle their full dues?

Answer:

- **Consistent Follow-Ups:** Set up a structured follow-up system with regular reminders about the remaining balance, and schedule check-ins to assess the customer's financial situation.

- **Escalate if Needed:** If partial payments continue, consider escalating to a higher-level collections agent or initiate formal actions like restructuring or legal escalation.

- **Analyse Payment Behaviour:** Use predictive analytics to understand why customers are making partial payments and consider offering them customized repayment plans.

16. What role does customer education play in the collections process?

Answer:

- **Financial Literacy Programs:** Educate customers about the importance of maintaining good credit, the consequences of missed payments, and how to budget effectively. This can help prevent future delinquencies.

- **Transparent Communication:** Be transparent about the loan terms, interest rates, and late payment penalties during onboarding and collections, reducing confusion or disputes later.

- **Interactive Communication:** Use easy-to-understand infographics and videos to explain complex terms related to the collections process.

17. How do we balance aggressive collections with maintaining customer relationships?

Answer:

- **Empathetic Collections:** Train agents to be empathetic, focusing on understanding the customer's situation and working together to find a resolution while being firm about obligations.

- **Escalation Protocols:** Use escalation only when necessary and ensure that initial contact is focused on building rapport and offering assistance rather than imposing consequences.

- **Incentivize Payments:** Offer incentives for prompt payments, such as discounts on interest rates or late fee waivers, to encourage timely repayments.

18. How do we manage and track settlements effectively?

Answer:

- **Clear Documentation:** Ensure that all settlement agreements are documented thoroughly and both parties agree on the terms before finalizing.

- **Payment Plan Monitoring:** Set up reminders and systems to track when settlement payments are due, ensuring that customers adhere to the agreed schedule.

- **Regular Communication:** Maintain ongoing communication with customers who have entered into settlements to ensure that they remain committed to the repayment plan.

19. What are the best practices for handling disputes regarding the amount owed?

Answer:

- **Thorough Review of Account History:** Always review the account history before engaging in a dispute resolution to ensure accuracy in the amount owed.

- **Third-Party Mediation:** If a dispute is complex, consider involving a third-party mediator or legal team to resolve disagreements in a fair and objective manner.

- **Clear Communication:** Provide customers with detailed statements showing all charges, payments, and adjustments, and offer them an opportunity to question or dispute the amounts.

20. How can collections teams effectively manage international collections?

Answer:

- **Local Regulations Awareness:** Ensure the collections team is familiar with the local regulations and collections practices in the countries where the debtors are located.

- **Cultural Sensitivity:** Train agents to understand and respect the cultural norms of international clients, adapting communication styles accordingly.

- **Global Network of Agencies:** Build relationships with trusted international debt collection agencies or third-party partners who understand local laws and practices to handle cross-border collections.

24

Common Challenges & How to Address Them

1. High Attrition Rates in Collections Teams

Problem: Attrition rates are often high due to burnout, stress, and lack of career growth.

Solution:

- **Motivation Strategies:** Introduce performance-based incentives, recognition programs, and regular feedback loops to boost morale.

- **Career Development:** Provide clear career progression paths, training, and skill development opportunities to agents.

- **Work-Life Balance:** Encourage a healthy work-life balance by offering flexible working hours or remote working options, especially for digital collections teams.

2. Low Recovery Rates

Problem: Low recovery rates may be caused by inefficient allocation of accounts or ineffective communication with customers.

Solution:

- **Enhanced Segmentation:** Implement better segmentation to focus efforts on high-risk or high-value customers.

- **Technology Utilization:** Leverage predictive analytics to forecast the likelihood of repayment and allocate resources more efficiently.

- **Customer Engagement:** Train agents to have empathetic and personalized conversations with customers, ensuring they understand the repayment process and options available.

3. Customers Not Responding to Contact Attempts

Problem: Accounts that become unresponsive can delay the recovery process and escalate to higher delinquency buckets.

Solution:

- **Skip Tracing:** Utilize skip tracing tools to locate and contact the customer through alternative channels (family members, employers, social media).

- **Multiple Channels:** Increase outreach attempts across multiple channels like emails, SMS, phone calls, and digital platforms.

- **Personalized Communication:** If automated messages are not yielding results, assign senior agents to reach out to customers with tailored communication.

4. Non-Compliance with Regulatory Guidelines

Problem: Failing to comply with regulations can lead to legal actions, fines, and reputational damage.

Solution:

- **Automated Compliance Checks:** Use compliance software that flags any activities that may breach legal guidelines such as RBI rules or customer privacy laws.

- **Training and Awareness:** Regularly train collections teams on regulatory changes, ensuring they understand the consequences of non-compliance.

- **Auditable Documentation:** Maintain clear records of all customer interactions, complaints, and resolutions to demonstrate adherence to compliance standards during audits.

5. Disputes with Customers Over the Amount Due

Problem: Disputes arise when customers disagree on the amount owed or the repayment terms.

Solution:

- **Clear Documentation:** Ensure that all communication and agreements with customers are clearly documented, including payment plans and any agreed-upon concessions.

- **Dispute Resolution Process:** Create a clear and efficient process for resolving disputes, including escalating cases to a senior manager or dispute resolution team when necessary.

- **Customer Service Integration:** Involve customer service teams to resolve issues related to misunderstandings or billing errors promptly.

6. Limited Agent Productivity

Problem: Agent performance may vary, leading to inconsistent results in collections.

Solution:

- **Performance Metrics:** Establish clear KPIs to track agent performance, such as recovery rates, contact rates, and resolution times.

- **Ongoing Training:** Offer regular training to improve negotiation skills, compliance knowledge, and customer engagement techniques.

- **Incentives:** Tie agent performance to rewards and incentives, providing motivation to meet and exceed targets.

7. Inadequate Use of Technology in Collections

Problem: Many collections teams still rely on outdated methods, reducing efficiency and effectiveness.

Solution:

- **Invest in Modern Technology:** Implement AI-driven predictive models for prioritizing accounts, CRM systems to track customer interactions, and automated messaging for quicker follow-ups.

- **Data Analytics:** Use data-driven insights to identify patterns in payment behaviour, helping to personalize collections strategies.

- **Integration of Channels:** Ensure all customer communication channels (phone, email, chat, etc.) are integrated into a single platform for seamless communication.

8. Challenges with High Volume Collections

Problem: Managing a large volume of delinquent accounts can overwhelm agents and lead to decreased efficiency.

Solution:

- **Automated Systems:** Implement automated diallers and communication tools to handle high volumes efficiently.

- **Segmented Approach:** Use data analytics to prioritize high-value or high-risk customers for immediate action while managing lower-risk accounts through automated reminders.

- **Workload Distribution:** Implement workload balancing tools to evenly distribute accounts among agents and ensure that no agent is overwhelmed.

9. Poor Performance Due to Lack of Proper Training

Problem: Agents may struggle with negotiations or compliance if they are not properly trained.

Solution:

- **Ongoing Training Programs:** Regularly conduct training sessions on soft skills (e.g., negotiation, empathy), compliance guidelines, and the latest collections strategies.

- **Role-Playing Scenarios:** Implement role-playing techniques where agents practice handling difficult cases, helping them become more adept at managing real-life situations.

- **Performance Reviews:** Regularly review agent performance and provide constructive feedback to address skill gaps.

10. Difficulty in Engaging High-Risk Customers

Problem: Customers with severe delinquencies or high risk of default may be more difficult to engage.

Solution:

- **Targeted Outreach:** Tailor your outreach strategy to these customers by offering personalized repayment solutions, such as settlements or refinancing options.

- **Legal Action Consideration:** If necessary, escalate these accounts to the legal department for further action. Ensure all communication is compliant with relevant laws.

- **Use of Technology:** Use predictive analytics to identify the right time and method for engagement, improving the chances of reaching high-risk customers.

11. Ineffective Handling of Grievances or Disputes

Problem: Disputes related to the amount owed, payment terms, or customer experiences may go unresolved, affecting recovery efforts.

Solution:

- **Clear Dispute Resolution Process:** Establish a formal grievance management system where disputes are logged, investigated, and resolved promptly.

- **Root Cause Analysis:** Identify the root causes of grievances (e.g., incorrect billing, misunderstanding of terms) and resolve these issues to prevent future disputes.

- **Escalation Path:** Set up an escalation process for unresolved grievances, ensuring that senior management can intervene when needed.

12. Slow Payment Processing and Delays

Problem: Customers may make payments, but the processing delays can hinder collections tracking and impact team performance.

Solution:

- **Automate Payment Processing:** Use online payment portals that automatically update customer accounts once payment is made.

- **Real-Time Updates:** Ensure that collections systems are integrated with payment platforms so that payment statuses are updated in real time.

- **Quick Acknowledgment:** Send immediate acknowledgment of payments made, including an updated statement showing the remaining balance.

13. Inadequate Communication Between Collections and Other Departments

Problem: Poor coordination between collections, customer service, and legal teams can lead to inefficiencies and missed opportunities.

Solution:

- **Integrated Systems:** Implement a centralized system that enables real-time communication and collaboration between departments.

- **Cross-Departmental Meetings:** Hold regular meetings between collections, customer service, and legal teams to discuss complex cases and align on strategies.

- **Knowledge Sharing:** Encourage sharing of insights from each department to inform decisions on how to approach collections for specific customers.

14. Inconsistent Adherence to Compliance Guidelines

Problem: Non-compliance with regulatory requirements can result in penalties, legal challenges, and damage to the organization's reputation.

Solution:

- **Compliance Automation:** Use compliance management tools that automatically monitor collections activities against regulatory requirements and flag potential violations.

- **Regular Audits:** Conduct regular internal and external audits to ensure that the collections process remains in line with applicable laws and regulations.

- **Compliance Training:** Ensure that all agents are regularly trained on the latest compliance guidelines, particularly those related to consumer protection laws.

15. Inconsistent Customer Data Across Systems

Problem: Having inconsistent or outdated customer data can lead to errors in collections and affect customer contact success.

Solution:

- **Data Integration:** Implement a central database that integrates information from all departments (sales, customer service, collections) to ensure a single source of truth.

- **Data Quality Checks:** Regularly conduct data quality audits to ensure that contact details and payment information are up to date.

- **Customer Consent for Updates:** Ensure that customers are aware of and consent to sharing updated information across platforms to maintain accurate records.

16. Poor Coordination Between Collections and Customer Service Teams

Problem: Lack of communication and coordination between collections and customer service teams can lead to inefficiencies and poor customer experience.

Solution:

- **Integrated Communication Platforms:** Use a unified CRM system that allows customer service and collections teams to access the same customer data and notes on each case.

- **Regular Coordination Meetings:** Hold monthly or quarterly meetings between collections and customer service teams to discuss current issues, upcoming strategies, and share insights.

- **Cross-Departmental Training:** Encourage training across departments so that collections agents understand customer service processes and vice versa.

17. Low Employee Morale Due to High Pressure or Unclear Expectations

Problem: High-pressure targets and unclear goals can lead to burnout and low morale among collections agents.

Solution:

- **Clear Targets and Realistic Goals:** Set clear, attainable targets that align with company objectives, but ensure they are realistic given the resources available.

- **Employee Recognition Programs:** Implement recognition programs for high performers, offering rewards like bonuses, additional time off, or public acknowledgment.

- **Regular Feedback and Support:** Create a culture of open communication where agents receive regular feedback and are encouraged to share any concerns or challenges.

18. Legal Issues or Compliance Violations in Collections

Problem: Violations of legal or regulatory requirements can result in fines, reputational damage, and legal consequences.

Solution:

- **Compliance Monitoring Tools:** Use automated tools to ensure that all collections efforts comply with local, national, and international regulations. These tools should provide alerts for potential compliance risks.

- **Regular Legal Training:** Provide ongoing training on local laws and regulations, particularly consumer protection laws, to avoid legal missteps during the collections process.

- **Documentation and Audit Trails:** Maintain clear, auditable records of all collections actions, including dates, communications, and resolutions, to defend against potential claims.

20. Inability to Handle High-Volume Collections Efficiently

Problem: When dealing with high volumes of delinquent accounts, it becomes increasingly difficult to manage and prioritize collections effectively.

Solution:

- **Tiered Collections Approach:** Implement a tiered approach where accounts are grouped based on risk, amount overdue, or age of delinquency. Focus efforts on high-value accounts and high-risk segments first.

- **Automated Outreach Systems:** Use automated communication tools to handle basic outreach for low-risk or early-stage delinquencies, while reserving human agents for high-priority cases.

- **Outsource or Co-Collect:** Consider outsourcing parts of the collections process to third-party agencies or using co-collection strategies for cases that are more difficult to resolve internally.

25

Glossary of Key Terms in Collections

Below is a detailed glossary of key terms commonly used in the collections process, as covered in this book. These terms are essential for understanding the strategies, metrics, and tools discussed in the context of collections in banking and financial service.

1. Account Coverage Ratio (ACR)

Definition: A metric used to measure the number of accounts assigned to a collections agent. It helps assess the efficiency and workload distribution for each agent.

Explanation: An ideal ACR ensures that an agent can handle a manageable number of accounts to maintain performance. For example, in higher-risk cases, a lower ACR ensures better focus and handling of each account.

2. Agent Productivity Metrics

Definition: Performance indicators that track the productivity of collections agents.

Explanation: These metrics include the number of accounts handled, the amount recovered per agent, and the number of successful contact attempts. Monitoring agent productivity helps in identifying areas for improvement and optimizing workflows.

3. BKT (Bucket)

Definition: A classification system used to categorize overdue accounts based on the length of time the payment has been delinquent.

Explanation: For example, BKT 1 could represent accounts that are 1-30 days overdue, while BKT 4 represents accounts that are 91-180 days overdue. The strategy for handling accounts varies by bucket.

4. Collection Efficiency

Definition: A measure of how effectively a collections team recovers overdue payments relative to the total outstanding obligation.

Explanation: Collection efficiency helps assess the overall performance of the collections team. High efficiency means that more overdue payments are being recovered, which directly impacts the financial stability of the institution.

5. Contact Success Rate (CSR)

Definition: The percentage of successful borrower contacts made out of the total attempts made by a collections agent.

Explanation: A high CSR indicates that the collections team is effectively reaching borrowers and can initiate repayment discussions. It's crucial for driving collections performance.

6. Collections Strategy

Definition: The structured approach a financial institution takes to recover overdue payments from borrowers.

Explanation: This includes defining processes, setting up KPIs, segmenting delinquent accounts, deciding on outreach strategies, and employing technology solutions to maximize collections efficiency.

7. Customer Relationship Management (CRM)

Definition: Software systems used to manage interactions with borrowers and maintain detailed records of customer interactions.

Explanation: A CRM system is key for tracking borrower history, follow-up schedules, and communications, ensuring a seamless collections experience and better customer engagement.

8. Early Delinquency (1–30 DPD)

Definition: The first stage of delinquency, where accounts are overdue by 1 to 30 days.

Explanation: During this stage, borrowers may be facing temporary financial issues. Early-stage collections typically involve reminders, payment plans, and gentle outreach.

9. First Contact Resolution (FCR)

Definition: The percentage of cases resolved during the first contact between the borrower and the collections agent.

Explanation: A high FCR rate indicates that the collections team is efficient in handling inquiries and resolving issues quickly, improving customer satisfaction and reducing follow-up efforts.

10. Grievance Redressal

Definition: The process of addressing and resolving complaints or issues raised by borrowers regarding their accounts or the collections process.

Explanation: Grievance redressal is an essential component of customer service in collections. It ensures borrowers' concerns are addressed promptly, reducing dissatisfaction and maintaining trust.

11. Promise-to-Pay (PTP) Conversion Rate

Definition: The percentage of borrowers who commit to a repayment plan and adhere to it.

Explanation: PTP conversion rates are critical for assessing how well the collections team is converting borrower promises into actual payments.

12. Recovery Rate

Definition: The percentage of the overdue amount that is successfully collected within a specified period.

Explanation: A higher recovery rate indicates better collections performance, and it is a key metric in evaluating the success of the collections strategy.

13. Reversal Rate

Definition: The percentage of accounts that were previously classified as delinquent and are later reverted to a current status due to a payment or resolution.

Explanation: A reversal rate shows how many accounts that were moved to a higher bucket (e.g., 90+ DPD) are brought back to a lower risk category due to successful collections or settlements.

14. Skip Tracing

Definition: The process of locating a borrower who has intentionally or unintentionally avoided being contacted.

Explanation: Skip tracing involves using various methods and tools to find borrowers who are unresponsive, ensuring collections efforts can continue even when borrowers are hard to reach.

15. Settlement Rate

Definition: The percentage of accounts resolved through settlements, where the borrower agrees to pay a reduced amount or renegotiate terms.

Explanation: The settlement rate measures the success of negotiated resolutions, which may be especially important for accounts in severe delinquency.

16. Total Outstanding (OD) Obligation

Definition: The total overdue amount for all accounts within a given collection portfolio.

Explanation: Monitoring OD obligations helps the collections team prioritize accounts and allocate resources efficiently based on the amount due for collection.

17. Write-Off Recovery Rate

Definition: The percentage of recovery achieved from accounts that were previously written off.

Explanation: Even after an account is written off, it's possible to recover a portion of the amount. A high write-off recovery rate is a sign of effective collections, even on bad debts.

18. Workflow Automation

Definition: The use of technology to streamline and automate various stages of the collections process, from contact attempts to payment processing.

Explanation: Automation improves efficiency, reduces human error, and helps the collections team focus on more complex tasks, such as negotiations and settlements.

19. Legal Action Conversion Rate

Definition: The percentage of accounts that are escalated to legal action or repossession after unsuccessful attempts to resolve the debt through standard collections methods.

Explanation: This rate indicates how often collections efforts have failed to resolve an account and how often legal action is necessary. It is a critical metric for risk management.

20. Regulatory Compliance

Definition: Adherence to the laws, regulations, and guidelines established by governing bodies (e.g., RBI, FCA) to ensure fair, ethical, and lawful collections practices.

Explanation: Compliance ensures that collections teams operate within legal boundaries, reducing the risk of fines, penalties, and reputational damage.

21. Skip Tracing Success Rate

Definition: The percentage of success in locating and contacting borrowers who have become unresponsive.

Explanation: This metric is important in assessing the effectiveness of skip tracing efforts, which help recover payments from borrowers who have intentionally or unintentionally avoided contact.

22. Account Rollback Rate

Definition: The percentage of accounts that are reverted from a higher risk category (e.g., 30–90 DPD) to a lower risk category (e.g., 1–30 DPD).

Explanation: A high rollback rate signifies that effective collections strategies are helping bring borrowers back to current status, thus preventing further deterioration of the account.

23. Collections Efficiency Ratio

Definition: A performance ratio that measures the effectiveness of the collections process in terms of total funds collected versus the resources expended.

Explanation: This ratio helps assess how well a collections team utilizes its resources (time, agents, technology) to recover overdue amounts. A high ratio indicates effective resource management and productivity.

24. Field Collections

Definition: The process of collecting overdue payments through in-person visits by collections agents.

Explanation: Field collections are typically used for high-risk accounts where digital or telephonic methods may have failed. It involves direct interaction with the borrower to negotiate payments or arrange settlements.

25. Digital Collections

Definition: The process of collecting overdue payments via digital channels such as emails, SMS, automated calling systems, and mobile apps.

Explanation: Digital collections are cost-effective and scalable. They are often employed in lower-risk cases where a borrower can be reached through automated messages or digital platforms.

26. Recovery Process

Definition: The set of procedures and activities involved in collecting overdue payments from delinquent borrowers.

Explanation: The recovery process includes communication with the borrower, setting repayment terms, escalating cases to higher management or legal channels, and executing final recovery actions such as settlement or repossession.

27. Residual Management

Definition: The process of managing residual balances or amounts that remain unpaid after the main debt has been settled or partially paid.

Explanation: In collections, residual management helps determine how to deal with outstanding amounts that may still be owed after an initial settlement or partial payment. It often involves setting up payment plans or negotiating additional settlements.

28. Debt Settlement

Definition: An agreement between the borrower and the creditor to settle a debt for less than the full amount owed.

Explanation: Debt settlement is typically used when a borrower is unable to repay the full amount and offers a reduced lump sum payment. It's often considered after multiple collection attempts or when legal action is imminent.

29. Charge-Off

Definition: The formal recognition that a debt is unlikely to be collected and is written off as a loss by the lender.

Explanation: When a debt is charged off, the bank or financial institution accepts that the loan is unlikely to be recovered. However, this does not absolve the borrower from the obligation to repay, and the collection process may continue.

30. Debt Restructuring

Definition: The process of modifying the terms of a borrower's loan to make repayment more manageable, often by extending the repayment period or lowering the interest rate.

Explanation: Debt restructuring is often used for borrowers facing temporary financial difficulties. It is a way to reduce defaults and provide an opportunity for the borrower to repay the debt under more favourable terms.

31. Repossessions

Definition: The act of reclaiming property (e.g., cars, homes) from a borrower due to non-payment.

Explanation: Repossession is often the final step in the collections process for secured loans, where the lender takes back the collateral to recover the outstanding loan amount. This action typically follows legal procedures and is used as a last resort.

32. Debt Recovery

Definition: The process of recovering the amount owed by a borrower who has defaulted on a loan.

Explanation: Debt recovery may involve contacting the borrower, negotiating settlements, and employing legal channels such as court orders or repossession.

33. Customer Service Level (CSL)

Definition: A measure of how well the collections team is providing service to customers during the collections process.

Explanation: CSL includes metrics like the time taken to respond to customer inquiries, resolution speed, and borrower satisfaction. It is essential for maintaining a positive relationship with borrowers while still pursuing collections.

34. Early Settlement

Definition: When a borrower repays part or all of the overdue amount before the due date, often in exchange for a discount or more favourable terms.

Explanation: Early settlement agreements can help improve cash flow and reduce the amount of bad debt for banks. It's an incentive for borrowers to resolve their debts quickly.

35. Risk Classification

Definition: The process of categorizing borrowers based on the likelihood of repayment or default.

Explanation: Risk classification is used to segment borrowers into different categories (e.g., low, medium, high risk). This allows the collections team to allocate resources effectively and apply tailored strategies for each group.

36. Threshold Limits

Definition: The specific balance or amount of overdue debt that triggers certain actions in the collections process.

Explanation: Threshold limits help banks determine when to escalate an account to a higher collection bucket or when to initiate legal or recovery actions. These limits are critical for streamlining the collections process and ensuring timely intervention.

37. Financial Hardship

Definition: A situation where a borrower is unable to meet their financial obligations due to unexpected circumstances, such as illness, job loss, or natural disasters.

Explanation: Borrowers experiencing financial hardship may be eligible for special repayment terms, such as temporary forbearance or loan restructuring. Collections teams must identify these situations early to avoid unnecessary escalation.

38. Internal Collections vs. External Agencies

Definition: Refers to the distinction between in-house collections teams within the bank and third-party collection agencies hired to recover debts.

Explanation: Internal collections teams are typically more familiar with the borrower's history and can handle sensitive cases. In contrast, external agencies are often used for accounts that have been severely delinquent or require specialized expertise in recovery.

39. Batch Collections

Definition: The process of handling multiple delinquent accounts in batches rather than individually.

Explanation: Batch collections help streamline the collections process, particularly in cases where the amounts owed are small or the borrowers are not responding to earlier attempts. It allows for more efficient management of high volumes of accounts.

40. Automated Collections System

Definition: A software system designed to manage and automate the collections process, including account monitoring, communication, and reporting.

Explanation: Automated collections systems use algorithms to prioritize accounts, schedule reminders, and send automated messages, reducing the workload on collections agents and ensuring consistent follow-up with borrowers.

41. Arrears

Definition: The amount of money that is overdue and has not yet been paid by the borrower.

Explanation: Arrears are a critical metric in collections, as they represent the total value of delinquent payments. Managing arrears is crucial for maintaining the health of the bank's portfolio and ensuring timely collections.

42. Account Normalization

Definition: The process of returning an overdue account to good standing after a borrower has made payment arrangements or settled their debt.

Explanation: Account normalization typically involves updating the borrower's credit status and removing negative marks from their record after they meet the agreed-upon repayment terms. It is a key indicator of successful collections.

43. Behavioural Scoring

Definition: A method used to assess a borrower's likelihood of default based on past payment behaviour and other risk factors.

Explanation: Behavioural scoring is an essential tool for prioritizing collections efforts. Borrowers with higher risk scores may receive more intensive collection efforts, while lower-risk borrowers may be offered more lenient repayment terms.

44. Loan Modification

Definition: The process of altering the terms of a loan agreement to make it easier for the borrower to repay.

Explanation: Loan modification may involve reducing interest rates, extending repayment periods, or changing the loan type. It's a tool used to prevent defaults and help borrowers who are struggling financially.

Certainly! Here is additional glossary terms related to collections:

45. Payment Plan

Definition: A structured arrangement between the lender and the borrower that outlines how the borrower will repay their debt over time.

Explanation: Payment plans are often used when a borrower is unable to pay the full amount at once. The plan may involve instalment payments over a set period, and it helps prevent accounts from moving into higher delinquency buckets.

46. Debt Collection Agency (DCA)

Definition: An external company or organization hired by a lender or creditor to recover overdue payments.

Explanation: DCAs specialize in pursuing delinquent borrowers who have failed to respond to in-house collections efforts. They typically use a variety of collection methods, including letters, phone calls, and legal action if necessary.

47. Collection Agent

Definition: An individual responsible for contacting borrowers to recover overdue payments.

Explanation: Collection agents can work for the bank or a third-party collection agency. They use communication skills to negotiate repayments, offer settlements, and create payment plans.

48. Bad Debt

Definition: A debt that is unlikely to be recovered due to the borrower's inability to repay or a long period of non-payment.

Explanation: Bad debt is usually written off by the bank, and it can negatively affect the institution's financial statements. Managing bad debt is a key focus of the collections process.

49. Charge-Off Account

Definition: An account that has been classified as uncollectible by the lender after a period of unsuccessful collections.

Explanation: A charge-off does not mean the debt is forgiven; it is an accounting entry where the bank acknowledges the debt as a loss. However, the borrower remains responsible for the debt, and collection efforts may continue.

50. Collection Threshold

Definition: The specific period of overdue payments or balance amount that triggers the initiation of the collections process.

Explanation: Collection thresholds help banks determine when accounts should be escalated to a collections team. For example, a bank might initiate collections after a borrower has been 30 days overdue on a loan.

51. Debt Recovery Agent

Definition: A professional tasked with recovering debts from borrowers, typically by contacting them, negotiating settlements, or taking legal action.

Explanation: Debt recovery agents work to retrieve funds for the creditor and often follow strict protocols to ensure compliance with laws and regulations governing collections practices.

52. Late Payment Fee

Definition: A charge applied to a borrower's account if they fail to make payments by the due date.

Explanation: Late payment fees are often a part of the collections strategy to encourage timely repayment. They may also serve as a penalty for non-payment, which may prompt borrowers to pay their overdue amounts.

53. Partial Payment

Definition: A payment made by the borrower that does not cover the full outstanding balance.

Explanation: Partial payments are common in collections, particularly for borrowers experiencing financial hardship. They can help reduce the debt but may also signal the need for further negotiations, such as restructuring or payment plan agreements.

54. High-Risk Borrowers

Definition: Borrowers who are more likely to default on their debt due to factors such as poor credit history, financial instability, or a history of late payments.

Explanation: High-risk borrowers require more intensive collections strategies. Banks may deploy additional resources, such as legal action or escalation to third-party agencies, to recover debts from high-risk individuals.

55. Delinquency Bucket

Definition: A classification system used to group accounts based on the length of time they have been overdue.

Explanation: Common buckets include 1–30 DPD (days past due), 31–60 DPD, 61–90 DPD, and so on. Each bucket represents increasing levels of risk and delinquency, with more aggressive collection methods applied as the bucket number increases.

56. Delinquent Account

Definition: An account where the borrower has failed to make a payment by the due date, resulting in an overdue balance.

Explanation: A delinquent account may be flagged for collections and moved into a higher delinquency bucket, which triggers a series of collection efforts to recover the overdue amount.

57. Co-Signer

Definition: An individual who agrees to take responsibility for repaying a loan if the primary borrower defaults.

Explanation: Co-signers are typically involved in collections when the primary borrower defaults. The bank may pursue the co-signer for repayment if the original borrower is unable to pay.

58. Debt Forgiveness

Definition: The cancellation of all or part of a borrower's outstanding debt.

Explanation: Debt forgiveness can occur in specific circumstances, such as after a borrower demonstrates extreme financial hardship. While it is not always a desirable outcome for banks, it may be used as a last resort to avoid a total write-off.

59. Pre-Collection

Definition: The phase before formal collection efforts begins, during which borrowers are reminded of their payment obligations.

Explanation: Pre-collection strategies often involve gentle reminders, such as email notifications or SMS alerts, to encourage timely payment before the account is escalated to formal collections procedures.

60. Regulatory Compliance in Collections

Definition: The adherence to laws, regulations, and industry standards governing the collections process.

Explanation: Regulatory compliance ensures that collection practices remain ethical and legal. Banks must ensure their collections teams are trained to follow the guidelines set by regulators, such as the RBI in India or the CFPB in the U.S.

61. Collections Compliance Officer

Definition: A person responsible for ensuring that all collections activities comply with relevant laws, regulations, and internal policies.

Explanation: The collections compliance officer plays a critical role in monitoring the collections process to ensure legal and ethical standards are met. They also conduct audits and training to reduce the risk of non-compliance.

62. Cross-Channel Collections

Definition: The use of multiple communication channels (e.g., phone, email, SMS, mobile apps) to contact borrowers for collections.

Explanation: Cross-channel collections strategies are used to reach borrowers through their preferred methods of communication, increasing the likelihood of successful repayment. This approach allows for a more personalized and effective collections process.

63. Collection Cycle

Definition: The series of steps or stages involved in the collections process, from initial contact to final resolution.

Explanation: A collection cycle includes several phases, such as account monitoring, borrower outreach, negotiations, and, if necessary, legal or recovery actions. The length and intensity of the cycle depend on the borrower's response and the severity of the delinquency.

64. Borrower Rehabilitation

Definition: The process of assisting a borrower in overcoming financial difficulties by restructuring their loan or offering support services.

Explanation: Borrower rehabilitation can involve modifying loan terms, offering financial counselling, or negotiating settlement options. The goal is to help the borrower return to financial stability and avoid default.

Abbreviations used in collections.

Abbreviation	Explanation
A/C	Account - Refers to the borrower's financial account with the institution from which a debt is owed.
ACR	Account Coverage Ratio - The ratio of accounts assigned to a collector compared to their capacity, ensuring effective management of cases.
AIP	Asset Identification Process - A process used to identify and recover assets that serve as collateral for a loan.
AR	Accounts Receivable - Money owed to a business or bank by customers for goods or services provided, often tracked for collections purposes.
ARAP	Accounts Receivable Aging Process - The process of categorizing overdue accounts based on how long the debts have been outstanding.
ARPU	Average Revenue Per User - A metric used to calculate the average income generated per borrower or customer, often used to assess profitability.
BKT	Bucket - Classification of overdue accounts by the number of days past due (e.g., 1–30 DPD, 31–60 DPD, 90+ DPD).
CBR	Credit Bureau Report - A detailed report that tracks a borrower's credit history, including payment habits and outstanding debts.

Abbreviation	Explanation
CCA	Credit Collection Agency - A third-party service provider hired by creditors to recover outstanding debts.
CCO	Chief Collections Officer - A senior executive responsible for overseeing the collections department, developing strategies, and ensuring compliance.
CFA	Consumer Financial Affairs - The division of a bank that manages consumer financial products, including collections on credit cards and personal loans.
CFD	Collection Focused Debt - A category of debt that requires targeted collection efforts due to its nature or the borrower's circumstances.
CIC	Credit Information Center - A bureau or organization that provides credit-related information, often used for collection-related decisions.
CIF	Customer Information File - A comprehensive file containing all pertinent information related to a customer's banking relationship.
CMR	Collection Management Ratio - The ratio between the collections achieved and the total outstanding balances in a portfolio.
CNF	Cash-N-Carry - A payment method where a borrower makes full payment in cash to complete a transaction or settlement of debt.

Abbreviation	Explanation
CRA	Credit Rating Agency - A firm that assigns credit ratings to debt issuers, helping institutions assess borrower risk.
CRO	Collections Recovery Officer - An individual responsible for managing and overseeing the recovery of overdue accounts.
DA	Debt Arrangement - The process by which a borrower and lender agree on a plan to repay the overdue debt.
DBR	Debt Burden Ratio - A metric used to measure the borrower's total monthly debt obligations in relation to their monthly income.
DC	Debt Collection - The process of collecting overdue payments from individuals or businesses who have defaulted on a loan.
DCO	Debt Collection Officer - A role responsible for overseeing collections activities, managing customer relations, and ensuring compliance with regulations.
DCR	Debt Collection Ratio - A metric that measures the percentage of overdue debt that has been successfully collected.
DMP	Debt Management Plan - A structured repayment plan arranged between the borrower and a financial institution or third-party agency.
DOS	Days of Sale - A metric used to track how long it takes to collect a debt after a sale or transaction.

Abbreviation	Explanation
DPA	Debt Payment Assistance - A program or service designed to help borrowers repay their debts, often involving restructuring terms or lower payments.
DPD	Days Past Due - The number of days a loan is overdue from its due date.
DPR	Debt Payment Ratio - A ratio indicating the proportion of income a borrower uses to repay debt.
EOD	End of Day - Refers to the daily closure of collection activities, typically to assess the performance, track final data, or finish necessary documentation.
EP	Escalation Process - A defined process where overdue cases are escalated to higher management for quicker resolution.
ER	Exposure Report - A report that provides a detailed view of the current outstanding debts, broken down by account type, loan type, and risk level.
FAT	Full and Final Settlement - An agreement where the borrower settles the entire debt for a reduced amount, often agreed upon as a one-time payment.
FC	Foreclosure - The legal process by which a lender takes control of a property from a borrower who has failed to make loan payments.

Abbreviation	Explanation
FCA	Financial Conduct Authority - A regulatory body in some countries responsible for overseeing financial institutions, including collections practices and compliance.
FCR	First Contact Resolution - Percentage of cases resolved during the first interaction with the borrower.
FRR	Fraud Recovery Rate - The percentage of fraudulent loans or accounts that have been successfully recovered or settled.
FSA	Financial Settlement Agreement - A legal agreement detailing the terms under which a borrower can settle their debt.
GA	Grievance Agent - A dedicated agent responsible for handling borrower complaints and disputes, ensuring a fair resolution process.
GRC	Grievance Redressal Committee - A committee responsible for addressing borrower complaints and grievances, ensuring issues are resolved in compliance with regulatory requirements.
HP	Hardship Program - A program designed to assist borrowers facing financial hardship by providing alternative repayment terms, often to prevent defaults.
IBR	Income-Based Repayment - A payment plan that ties the borrower's monthly loan payments to their income, helping those in financial difficulty.

Abbreviation	Explanation
IRR	Internal Rate of Return - A metric used to measure the profitability of investments, including loan portfolios.
IVR	Interactive Voice Response - A technology that allows customers to interact with automated banking systems via telephone, commonly used for repayment reminders or customer queries.
KYC	Know Your Customer - A process used by financial institutions to verify the identity of their clients to prevent fraud and money laundering.
LB	Late Borrower - A borrower who has missed one or more payment deadlines and is now in arrears.
LCA	Loan Collection Agency - A third-party agency hired by the lender to collect overdue debts.
LOA	Letter of Authority - A legal document granting authority to a third party to act on behalf of the lender in pursuing debt recovery.
LPA	Loan Payment Arrangement - An agreement between the borrower and lender to make regular payments toward a loan over an extended period.
LPD	Loan Payment Default - Occurs when a borrower fails to make a scheduled payment on their loan.

Abbreviation	Explanation
LPI	Late Payment Interest - The interest charged on overdue payments or accounts.
LTV	Loan to Value - The ratio of the loan amount to the appraised value of the collateral.
MOU	Memorandum of Understanding - A formal agreement between parties outlining the terms and conditions of a debt recovery process or settlement arrangement.
NBFC	Non-Banking Financial Company - A financial institution that provides banking services without meeting the legal definition of a bank.
NDC	Non-Debt Collection - A collection strategy that involves non-debt instruments such as asset recovery.
NPA	Non-Performing Asset - A loan or asset that is in default or not generating the expected income, posing a risk to the bank.
NPL	Non-Performing Loan - A loan in which the borrower is not making scheduled payments, typically classified after a certain period of non-payment.
OC	Outstanding Collection - Refers to the value of unpaid debt that needs to be collected.
OCC	Overdue Customer Contact - A metric that tracks the number of customers who have been contacted regarding overdue payments.
OD	Overdue - Refers to an account balance that has not been paid by the due date.

Abbreviation	Explanation
OOS	Out of Service - Refers to accounts or customers that cannot be contacted or have been temporarily removed from the collection process.
OTS	One-Time Settlement - A special arrangement where the borrower settles their debt in a single payment, often for a reduced amount.
PD	Provision for Doubtful Debt - An accounting method used to estimate the amount of a lender's loans that are unlikely to be repaid.
PDC	Post-Dated Cheque - A cheque written with a future date, often used by borrowers as a commitment to pay the lender on a later date.
PDL	Payday Loan - A type of short-term, high-interest loan typically due on the borrower's next payday.
PF	Payment Facility - A method or platform provided by the lender to facilitate borrower payments, such as online portals or mobile apps.
PSA	Payment Settlement Agreement - An agreement that outlines the terms under which a borrower can settle their debt.
PTP	Promise to Pay - The borrower's commitment to repay a certain amount on a loan, typically made during an interaction or call.

Abbreviation	Explanation
PTP Rate	Promise-to-Pay Conversion Rate - The percentage of borrowers who make a payment commitment and honour it.
RBI	Reserve Bank of India - India's central banking institution, which issues guidelines and policies related to collections and lending practices.
RBL	Recovery Balance - The remaining amount owed by a borrower after partial payments have been made.
RC	Recovery Channel - The method or route used to recover a debt, such as through legal action, settlements, or asset recovery.
RCA	Root Cause Analysis - The process of identifying the underlying causes of persistent collection issues, such as poor payment behaviour or frequent delinquencies.
REFI	Refinancing - The process of replacing an old loan with a new one, typically to achieve more favourable terms for the borrower or lender.
RFC	Request for Collection - A formal request to a collection agency or internal team to initiate debt recovery efforts.
RFS	Recovery and Fraud Services - A division or team focused on recovering lost assets due to fraud and managing debt collection activities.

Abbreviation	Explanation
ROA	Recovery of Assets - The process of retrieving assets pledged by the borrower in case of loan default.
ROE	Resolution of Escalation - A measure of how effectively high-risk or complex collection cases are escalated and resolved.
RP	Recovery Plan - A structured strategy for recovering debts from delinquent borrowers.
RPC	Right Party Contact - Percentage of borrowers successfully contacted out of the total number of outreach attempts.
RPV	Recovery Potential Value - The estimated value that can be recovered from a delinquent loan or asset.
RRR	Restructuring and Recovery Ratio - A metric used to measure the effectiveness of loan restructuring efforts, comparing the amount recovered to the amount restructured.
RV	Recovery Value - The amount recovered from a debtor, particularly from assets used to secure a loan.
SL	Settlement Letter - A document issued by the lender confirming that a loan has been settled, often at a reduced amount.
SLA	Service Level Agreement - A contract between the collections department and external service providers that specifies the expected level of service.

Abbreviation	Explanation
SPOC	Single Point of Contact - A dedicated agent or team that serves as the primary contact for handling borrower issues or collections.
SRR	Settlement Recovery Rate - Percentage of accounts resolved through settlement or restructuring.
SV	Settlement Value - The amount agreed upon between the borrower and lender to settle a debt.
TAP	Temporary Account Payment - A short-term payment arrangement for a borrower struggling to meet full repayment terms.
TAT	Turnaround Time - The time taken to complete a task, such as resolving an overdue account or making a contact attempt.
TDR	Temporary Debt Restructuring - A short-term modification of loan terms offered to borrowers facing temporary financial difficulties.
TL	Team Leader - An individual who manages and supervises a team of agents, ensuring collections performance and process adherence.
TRR	Total Recovery Rate - The total amount recovered from overdue debts, including both principal and interest, compared to the total amount at risk.
VLR	Voluntary Liquidation Recovery - A recovery process where a borrower voluntarily liquidates assets to pay off debt.

26

Summary of "The Science of Collections"

"The Science of Collections" is a holistic guide that bridges the art and science of collections management within the banking and financial services industry. Drawing from decades of expertise, the book dissects the complexities of collections, offering an intricate roadmap for practitioners to navigate this critical domain. Starting with the foundational principles of collections, it meticulously explores advanced strategies, data utilization, and operational frameworks essential for ensuring high recovery rates while maintaining customer trust and compliance.

The book begins by setting the stage with an overview of the collections landscape, emphasizing its importance as a strategic function that ensures financial stability and portfolio health. It then moves into the science behind collections, showcasing how data-driven decision-making and predictive analytics play pivotal roles in forecasting delinquency, segmenting portfolios, and formulating targeted recovery strategies.

Key topics such as **Portfolio Bifurcation, Logical Allocation of Accounts**, and **Maintaining Account Coverage Ratios (ACRs)** are thoroughly explored, providing insights into optimizing resource deployment. The book also emphasizes the power of **Automation in Collections**, offering practical solutions to enhance efficiency and accuracy while reducing human error.

Special focus is given to actionable frameworks like **Pre-Delinquency Management (PDM)** and **Bucket Strategies (X, Early Delinquency, and Hard Bucket)**, presenting tailored approaches for addressing different stages of delinquency. These strategies are supplemented by an in-depth discussion on **Repossession Management** and **Cross-Functional Collaboration**, highlighting the importance of teamwork among collections, legal, and customer service departments.

The integration of advanced technologies, such as AI-powered systems, predictive analytics, and automation tools, forms the backbone of the book's discussion on transforming collections. These technologies enable organizations to scale operations, optimize processes, and maintain compliance effortlessly. Regulatory adherence is also a key theme, with comprehensive guidance on navigating RBI guidelines and global standards.

Leadership principles are woven throughout the book, providing actionable insights into building and leading high-performing teams. The focus on team motivation, retention, and leveraging both field and digital agents ensures that organizations can sustain productivity and morale even in challenging scenarios.

Real-world case studies and examples bring these concepts to life, illustrating how organizations have successfully implemented these strategies to achieve measurable results.

By addressing FAQs, common challenges, and troubleshooting scenarios, the book also serves as a practical reference for day-to-day collections operations.

Key Takeaways from "The Science of Collections"

1. **Data and Strategy as Cornerstones:** The book underscores the importance of leveraging data analytics to predict delinquency, segment customers, and tailor strategies. A robust collections framework is grounded in precise data utilization and actionable insights.

2. **Intelligent Allocation and Resource Management:** Logical account allocation and maintaining the right Account Coverage Ratio (ACR) are highlighted as critical to improving productivity. These measures ensure that field agents and supervisors focus their efforts effectively on high-priority cases.

3. **Early Intervention and Proactivity:** Pre-Delinquency Management (PDM) is emphasized as a proactive measure that minimizes risk while enhancing customer relationships, reducing the likelihood of delinquency.

4. **Customized Bucket Strategies:** The book provides detailed strategies for each stage of delinquency, from Bucket X to hard buckets, ensuring that collection efforts are optimized for maximum recovery while minimizing operational costs.

5. **Technology as a Game-Changer:** Advanced analytics, AI-powered voice and chatbots, and automation are shown to revolutionize collections. These tools

enhance efficiency, accuracy, and scalability, enabling organizations to meet evolving challenges head-on.

6. **The Role of Collaboration:** Seamless integration between collections, legal, customer service, and other functions is critical for effective recovery and compliance. The book presents frameworks to foster this collaboration and reduce process bottlenecks.

7. **Leadership and Team Building:** Building and sustaining high-performance teams is a recurring theme. Strategies to motivate, train, and retain field and digital agents are shared, ensuring that team morale and productivity remain consistently high.

8. **Regulatory Compliance as a Priority:** A strong emphasis is placed on aligning collections practices with RBI guidelines and global regulatory standards. This ensures risk mitigation, enhances trust, and maintains an organization's reputation.

9. **Future-Ready Collections:** Preparing for the future is a central theme. Adapting to changing market dynamics, addressing evolving customer expectations, and integrating ESG (Environmental, Social, Governance) principles into collections practices are discussed in detail.

10. **Case Studies as Learning Tools:** Real-world examples and use cases demonstrate the practical implementation of strategies and technologies, offering readers tangible insights and solutions for similar challenges in their organizations.

Final Thoughts

"The Science of Collections" is a vital resource for professionals seeking to transform collections into a strategic advantage. By integrating data, technology, strategy, and leadership, the book equips readers with the tools needed to navigate the complexities of collections management. Whether you are a collections manager, strategist, or leader, this book offers actionable insights, innovative solutions, and a vision for the future of collections. It redefines collections not as a reactive function but as a cornerstone of financial health, sustainability, and customer trust.

27

Acknowledgment and Gratitude

This book is a culmination of years of experience, relentless learning, and the unwavering support of those who have been a part of my journey.

First and foremost, I extend my heartfelt gratitude to my brother, **Balaji**, for being a guiding light and a source of wisdom throughout my life. To my wife, **Nishmaja**, your unwavering belief in me and steadfast support have been the cornerstone of my career and achievements.

I fondly remember my school friends—**Manju**, **Vinod**, **Jana**, and others—whose friendships have added strength and joy to my life. To my few but cherished personal friends, **Gopi and Pappan**, and my close collaborators from the TATA days, **Valentine and Sayantan Roy**, thank you for your camaraderie and critical insights that enriched my professional growth.

A special acknowledgment goes to my mentor at Tata Motors Finance, **Mr. Alok Chadha**, whose guidance and wisdom have profoundly shaped my career and professional outlook.

Finally, I thank my colleagues, mentors, family, and friends who have supported me through every challenge and success. Your belief in me is reflected in every chapter of this book. Thank you all for being an integral part of this journey.

This book reflects my journey and learnings from 25 years in the banking industry. To ensure a smooth and polished reading experience, I have relied on tools like Copilot for creating images and ChatGPT for refining the language and enhancing sentence structure. While these tools have helped in presentation, the ideas, strategies, and experiences are entirely my own.

— Vijay Vasudevan